COZY COTTAGE & CABIN DESIGNS

200+ Cottages, Cabins, A-Frames, Vacation Homes, Apartment Garages, Sheds & More

CRE▲TIVE
HOMEOWNER®

Book content provided by Design America, Inc., St. Louis, MO.

Creative Homeowner Project Team
Vice President-Content: Christopher Reggio
Editor: Anthony Regolino
Designer: Christopher Morrison

ISBN 978-1-58011-841-5

Library of Congress Control Number:2019945995

We are always looking for talented authors. To submit an idea, please send a brief inquiry to acquisitions@foxchapelpublishing.com.

Printed in Singapore

Current Printing (last digit)
10 9 8 7 6 5 4 3 2

Creative Homeowner®, *www.creativehomeowner.com*, is an imprint of New Design Originals Corporation and distributed exclusively in North America by Fox Chapel Publishing Company, Inc., 800-457-9112, 903 Square Street, Mount Joy, PA 17552, and in the United Kingdom by Grantham Book Service, Trent Road, Grantham, Lincolnshire, NG31 7XQ.

On the Cover: Plan #C19-008D-0159 is featured on page 81, photo courtesy of designer/architect.

Let *Cozy Cottage & Cabin Designs* allow you to escape to that special place; the perfect small home placed in your favorite setting. Whether high atop a mountain, nestled along a lake shore, or situated on a sandy beach, all of the dwellings in this book are small homes designed for efficiency with each and every one having 1,200 total square feet or less of living area. Browse the floor plans, and find the ideal home that embraces everything you need for a comfortable and tranquil haven.

TABLE OF CONTENTS

WHAT MAKES A GREAT VACATION HOME?

The sound of waves crashing in the distance, or the gentle rustle of fall leaves making their way to the ground. Whichever sight or sound beckons you to take time away from your everyday life and discover a life less stressed, seek that special place. Most people can immediately picture the perfect setting that soothes their soul and takes them to a place where they instantly feel more at peace. But, besides the outdoor setting for the perfect getaway home, what features make it a great vacation getaway?

ENHANCE THE EXPERIENCE OF LIVING IN A SPECIAL PLACE

EASY ACCESS
Expansive decks that surround an entire home like the one shown to the right and below, provide easy access outdoors from any room. This allows homeowners to feel unified with their surroundings, which is almost always the main attraction in these special getaways.

RUSTIC, COZY TOUCHES
Also, the use of stone and dark wood trim creates a feeling of rustic charm. Warm and cozy, guests will never want to leave their surroundings when decorated with these details. Or, build a stone fireplace that adorns the main living space. Not only will it be beautiful, but it can provide an alternative heat source that will be sure to draw people in.

LIGHT & BRIGHT

Large dormer and picture windows make taking in views easy. Large windows offer a classic, alpine retreat compelling views, while still making the home feel like a private oasis tucked high in the mountains.

SEAMLESS TO THE OUTDOORS

A covered deck, like the one shown to the right below, is a great outdoor retreat. Perfect for alfresco meals, it allows outdoor enjoyment without the intensity of direct sunlight, making it perfect for sunbelt regions, beach, or coastal homes with tropical temperatures practically all year-round.

BREEZY BEDROOMS

Well-lit bedrooms with oversized windows not only permit sunlight, but help stir beach front breezes into interior spaces. With the use of beach accents, a bedroom like the one below is a cheerful, sunny retreat.

Many of these characteristics allow the natural beauty that surrounds your vacation home to shine.

Whether it's a cozy stone fireplace, a shaded covered deck, or a breezy beachside bedroom, these features will take your vacation home to a new level of relaxation and tranquility and lure you back time and time again.

CABINS

Plan #C19-163D-0004 is found on page 16.

Often blending perfectly with nature, cabins evoke a feeling of smaller, rustic living that works especially well in the rugged outdoor wilderness. Whether tucked close to a soothing stream or placed high in the snowy mountaintops, a cabin is the ideal small dwelling for getting away from it all. Typically, simple in style and decor, a cabin will always feel inviting and offer the perfect escape from everyday reality. Whether you're cozied up by the fireplace, or roasting marshmallows over an outdoor fire pit, cabin life will definitely create fond memories and moments of complete and total relaxation.

YELTON CABIN

If you're looking for a small, modern dwelling, or would love to escape city life but still have all of the amenities, then the Yelton cabin is for you. Soaring ceilings overhead will keep your special escape bright and cheerful. The openness promotes fun and easy entertaining when friends are over. You will be thankful for the large covered porch for those days when there's a mist in the air. This small home is far from boring and has everything you want!

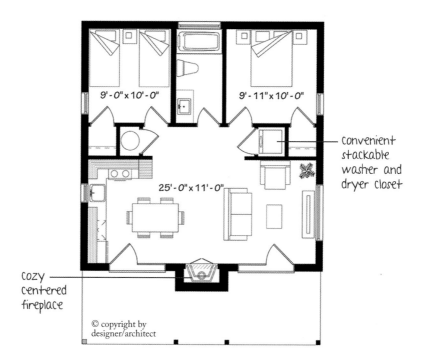

9'-0"x10'-0"

9'-11"x10'-0"

convenient
stackable
washer and
dryer closet

25'-0"x11'-0"

cozy
centered
fireplace

© copyright by
designer/architect

PLAN #C19-032D-0813

686 square feet of living area
width: 26' depth: 26'
2 bedrooms, 1 bath
2" x 6" exterior walls
monolithic slab foundation standard;
crawl space or floating slab available for a fee

BABLER CABIN

The Babler cabin rises to the challenge of housing up to eight people in a compact home. Step in from the covered front porch and find storage cabinets to the right and a bath/utility room to the left. In the center of the dwelling is the sitting/dining area with a vaulted 11' ceiling for added spaciousness. A wood-burning stove keeps the inside nice and cozy. The kitchenette handles uncomplicated meals with ease. The bunk room has enough space for four bunk beds, sleeping up to 8 people comfortably. This is a great cabin, perfect for family gatherings!

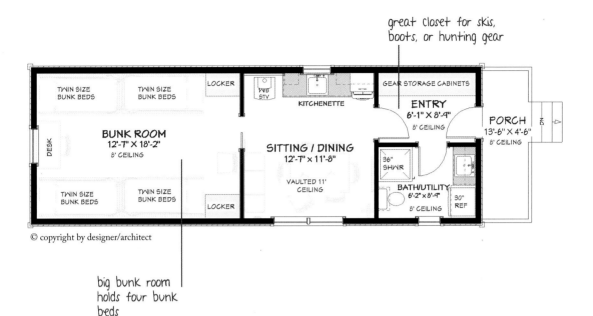

great closet for skis, boots, or hunting gear

LOCKER

TWIN SIZE BUNK BEDS   TWIN SIZE BUNK BEDS

W/D STV

GEAR STORAGE CABINETS

KITCHENETTE

DESK

BUNK ROOM
12'-7" X 18'-2"
8' CEILING

ENTRY
6'-1" X 8'-9"
8' CEILING

PORCH
13'-6" X 4'-6"
8' CEILING

TWIN SIZE BUNK BEDS   TWIN SIZE BUNK BEDS

SITTING / DINING
12'-7" x 11'-8"

VAULTED 11' CEILING

36" SHWR

LOCKER

BATH/UTILITY
6'-2" x 8'-9"
8' CEILING

30" REF

© copyright by designer/architect

big bunk room holds four bunk beds

PLAN #C19-135D-0005

559 square feet of living area
width: 13'-6"   depth: 44'-10"
1 bedroom, 1 bath
2" x 6" exterior walls
crawl space foundation

REDMOND PARK CABIN

Feel like you've really escaped the hustle and bustle in this rustic Redmond Park cabin featuring a multi-purpose living/dining room that is up to the challenges of evolving cabin activities. Designed for relaxed living, this cabin enjoys access all around its perimeter onto a large wraparound deck. Setup your grill on one side of the deck, and designate an area to sunbathe on the other. Plus, the second floor studio will make a perfect artist's retreat, home office, or a private escape great for taking in views from a private outdoor balcony.

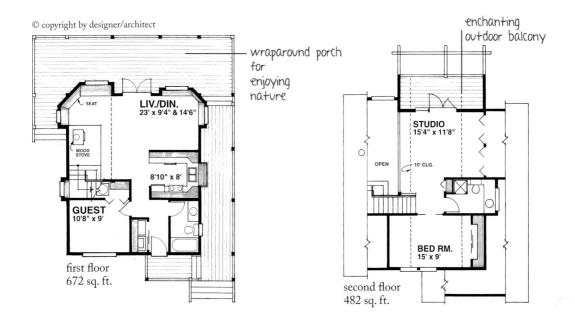

enchanting outdoor balcony

wraparound porch for enjoying nature

LIV./DIN.
23' x 9'4" & 14'6"

SEAT

WOOD STOVE

8'10" x 8'

GUEST
10'8" x 9'

first floor
672 sq. ft.

STUDIO
15'4" x 11'8"

OPEN

10' CLG.

BED RM.
15' x 9'

second floor
482 sq. ft.

PLAN #C19-080D-0004

1154 square feet of living area
width: 36'   depth: 42'-6"
2 bedrooms, 2 baths
2" x 6" exterior walls
crawl space foundation

CUB CREEK CABIN

Live a life of leisure in the Cub Creek cabin. Craftsman details give this small home tons of personality. Enjoy your morning coffee on the roomy covered porch, or grill up some burgers when it's time to barbecue. Inside, you'll find an open gathering space with a fireplace and many large windows for enjoying surrounding views. After a busy day in the wilderness, retreat to the comfortable bedrooms, each with their own bath.

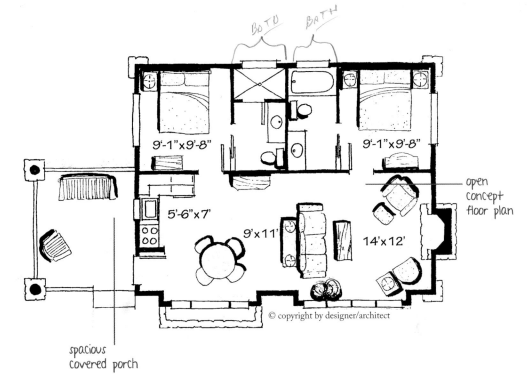

BDTD BATH

9'-1"x9'-8"

9'-1"x9'-8"

open
concept
floor plan

5'-6"x7'

9'x11'

14'x12'

© copyright by designer/architect

spacious
covered porch

PLAN #C19-163D-0004

681 square feet of living area
width: 40'   depth: 22'
2 bedrooms, 1 bath
2" x 6" exterior walls
crawl space or slab foundation,
please specify when ordering

PARSON PEAK CABIN

You'll never want to leave the Parson Peak rustic cabin. The open interior has tons of windows for admiring surrounding views. Two bedrooms are near a full bath with a freestanding tub and a walk-in shower for added and unexpected luxury. Those sitting at the sizable island in the kitchen can easily keep up with what is going on in the great room. And, if you suddenly want to venture outside, then the quiet deck off the back is easily accessible and will be the place for you.

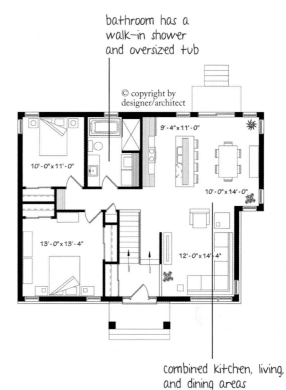

bathroom has a walk-in shower and oversized tub

© copyright by designer/architect

9'-4" x 11'-0"

10'-0" x 11'-0"

10'-0" x 14'-0"

13'-0" x 13'-4"

12'-0" x 14'-4"

combined kitchen, living, and dining areas

PLAN #C19-032D-0835

1146 square feet of living area
width: 40'   depth: 30'
2 bedrooms, 1 bath
2" x 6" exterior walls
basement foundation

MARKHALL CABIN

The Markhall cabin's two entry doors on the wraparound covered front porch are special features that allow guests and family to mingle easily from the porch to the interior. The large and open living room creates a great place for gathering. The center island in the kitchen offers extra dining space as well as a functional spot for preparing or serving meals. The dining room has several windows for a cheerful interior. The oversized corner whirlpool tub is comfortable and serene in the full bath. Although small, the Markhall cabin has everything you need!

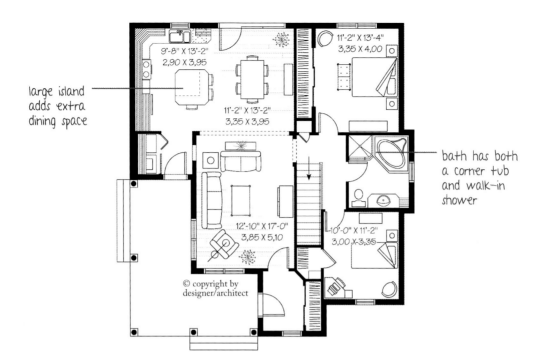

large island
adds extra
dining space

9'-8" X 13'-2"
2,90 X 3,95

11'-2" X 13'-2"
3,35 X 3,95

11'-2" X 13'-4"
3,35 X 4,00

bath has both
a corner tub
and walk-in
shower

12'-10" X 17'-0"
3,85 X 5,10

10'-0" X 11'-2"
3,00 X 3,35

© copyright by
designer/architect

PLAN #C19-032D-0656

1184 square feet of living area
width: 36'   depth: 40'
2 bedrooms, 1 bath
2" x 6" exterior walls
basement foundation standard; crawl space,
monolithic slab, or floating slab available for a fee

RHAPSODY CABIN

The Rhapsody cabin offers a quaint covered porch that greets guests as they arrive and provides a cozy area to sit and enjoy the smells and sounds of the surrounding outdoors. Spacious rooms throughout this home create a casual and open atmosphere. The kitchen and dining area combine for easy entertaining, and they are just steps away from the living room. The master suite on the second floor provides a private oasis that is sure to be appreciated by the homeowners.

© copyright by designer/architect

BA 2

BEDRM 2
8-10 x 9-4

UP

LIVING
13-8 x 15-2

large, open living space

KITCHEN
7-6 x 9-4

COV'D PORCH

DINING
9-4 x 9-4

first floor
650 sq. ft.

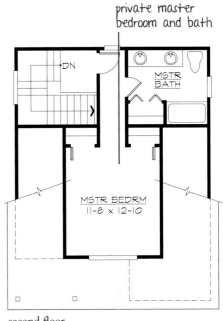

private master bedroom and bath

DN

MSTR BATH

MSTR BEDRM
11-8 x 12-10

second floor
350 sq. ft.

PLAN #C19-071D-0014

1000 square feet of living area
width: 24'   depth: 30'
2 bedrooms, 2 baths
2" x 6" exterior walls
crawl space foundation

CHICKADEE CABIN

Take time out at the Chickadee cabin. Whether lakeside or built in the mountains, cabin living in the Chickadee will not disappoint. Unwind on the large covered porch, which offers tons of covered outdoor space for staying cool in the shade. Inside, a pleasingly open layout makes mealtimes enjoyable with a communal feel. Two bedrooms provide a restful spot for a good night's sleep, and they are both handy to a centered bathroom. If you need to do a load of laundry, then the closet for a stackable washer and dryer is not hard to reach. Life will be easygoing in this cabin!

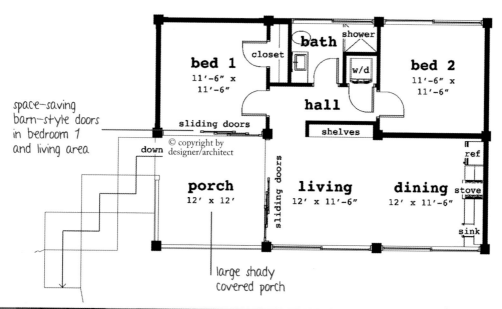

bed 1
11'-6" x
11'-6"

closet

bath

shower

w/d

bed 2
11'-6" x
11'-6"

hall

shelves

space-saving
barn-style doors
in bedroom 1
and living area

sliding doors

© copyright by
designer/architect

down

porch
12' x 12'

sliding doors

living
12' x 11'-6"

dining
12' x 11'-6"

ref

stove

sink

large shady
covered porch

PLAN #C19-152D-0115

750 square feet of living area
width: 37'   depth: 25'
2 bedrooms, 1 bath
2" x 6" exterior walls
pilings or crawl space foundation,
please specify when ordering

PARSON GROVE CABIN

Enjoy the beauty of the backwoods in the Parson Grove cabin. With its expansive covered front porch, sitting around after a day of fishing or hiking will be a pleasure there. You'll be amazed when you step inside and discover the vaulted great room creating such a spacious feel to the interior. The kitchen with an eating bar for five people is entirely open to the great room, too. Everyone will be thankful for the cozy fireplace. Even though this cabin is small, it provides great comfort and function.

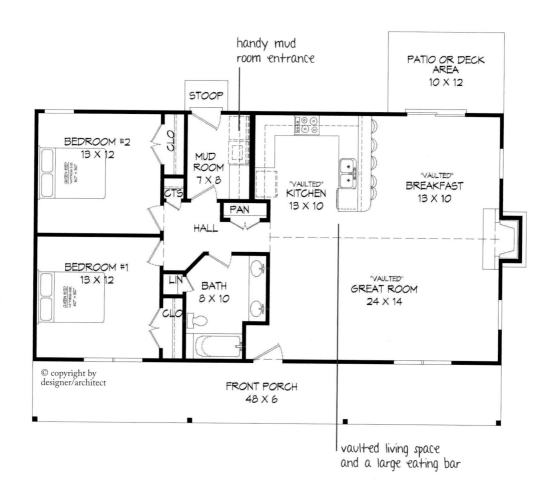

handy mud
room entrance

PATIO OR DECK
AREA
10 X 12

STOOP

BEDROOM #2
13 X 12

CLO

MUD
ROOM
7 X 8

CTS

"VAULTED"
KITCHEN
13 X 10

"VAULTED"
BREAKFAST
13 X 10

PAN

HALL

BEDROOM #1
13 X 12

LIN

BATH
8 X 10

"VAULTED"
GREAT ROOM
24 X 14

CLO

© copyright by
designer/architect

FRONT PORCH
48 X 6

vaulted living space
and a large eating bar

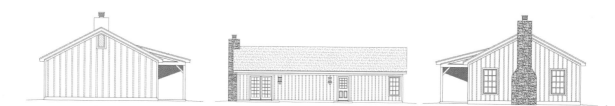

PLAN #C19-141D-0013

1200 square feet of living area
width: 50'   depth: 33'
2 bedrooms, 1 bath
2" x 6" exterior walls
slab foundation

CROSSWOOD CABIN

The Crosswood cabin is an excellent starter home for any family. The living room boasts a handy coat closet located near the front entry. The efficient kitchen/dining area includes a side entrance to the outdoors, a closet that is perfect for a pantry, and a convenient laundry closet, so there is not a shortage in storage! The lovely master bedroom features a walk-in closet and private access to the bath. There sure is a lot of function for a smaller-size home!

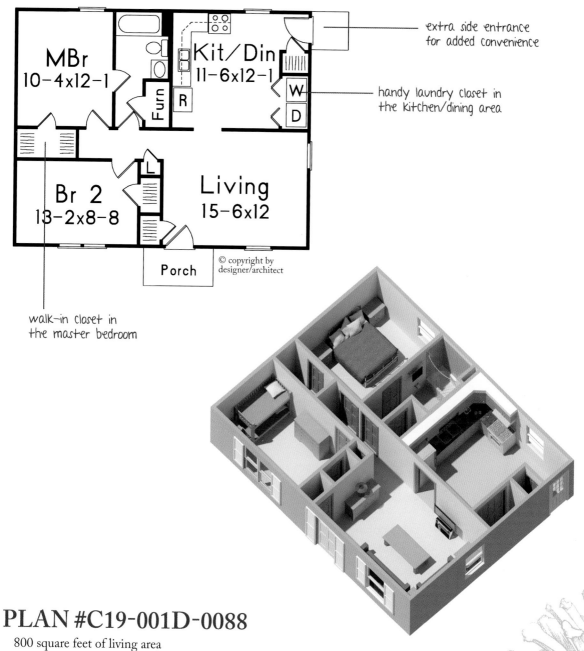

MBr
10-4x12-1

Kit/Din
11-6x12-1

extra side entrance
for added convenience

handy laundry closet in
the kitchen/dining area

Furn

W
D
R

Br 2
13-2x8-8

Living
15-6x12

walk-in closet in
the master bedroom

Porch

© copyright by
designer/architect

PLAN #C19-001D-0088

800 square feet of living area
width: 32'   depth: 25'
2 bedrooms, 1 bath
crawl space foundation standard;
slab available for a fee

CHRISTY MEADOW CABIN

Rustic cabin living was never as comfortable as it is in the Christy Meadow cabin thanks to its very open floor plan, a front covered porch, and a rear covered patio. The conveniently located master bedroom has a walk-in closet, covered porch views, and direct access into the bathroom. Two additional bedrooms are located on the second floor.

PLAN #C19-111D-0033

1157 square feet of living area
width: 36'   depth: 38'
3 bedrooms, 2 baths
slab foundation standard;
crawl space or basement available for a fee

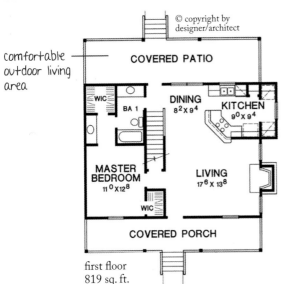

comfortable outdoor living area

first floor
819 sq. ft.

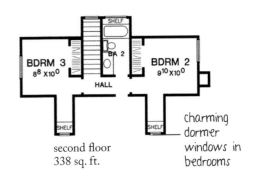

second floor
338 sq. ft.

charming dormer windows in bedrooms

CATHY CREEK CABIN

PLAN #C19-111D-0032

1094 square feet of living area
width: 40'   depth: 37'-6"
3 bedrooms, 2 baths
slab foundation standard;
crawl space or basement available for a fee

Rustic style at its finest in the Cathy Creek cabin. Breathe easy on the front covered wraparound porch with stairs that lead to a detached garage. Blended spaces create an area that feels larger than its true size. Three bedrooms provide enough space for family comfort.

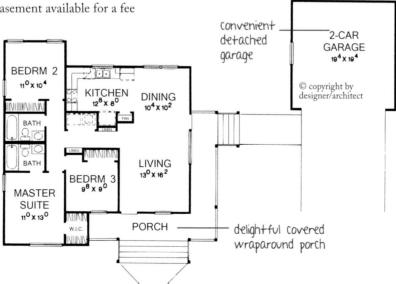

RIVER'S EDGE CABIN

PLAN #C19-155D-0100

970 square feet of living area
width: 24' depth: 56'-6"
3 bedrooms, 1 bath
crawl space or slab foundation,
please specify when ordering

Life in the River's Edge cabin will be harmonious. There's plenty of space for everyone with its three bedrooms and centrally placed bathroom. Barbecue time will be a thrill on your very own grilling porch. After grilling, settle into the screened entry porch and dine outdoors free of pests. The living and dining spaces are vaulted for a more open feel. The kitchen has a sizable laundry room nearby providing additional storage and space for chores. Whether a weekend escape, or a year-round residence, the River's Edge promises a life less hassled.

© copyright by designer/architect

GRILLING PORCH
10'-8" X 10'-7"

large laundry room

LAU.
9'-10" X 8'-6"

PANTRY

BEDROOM 3
13' X 9'-9"

REF

DW

KIT
10' X 10'-7"

RG

BEDROOM 2
9'-2" X 9'-4"

BATH
9'-2" X 5'

DINING
9' X 8'

LIVING
13'-8" X 12'

BEDROOM 1
9'-2" X 11'-10"

VAULTED CEILING

SCREENED ENTRY PORCH
15' X 8'

screened porch, perfect for dining

PROVIDER II CABIN

PLAN #C19-001D-0040

864 square feet of living area
width: 36'   depth: 28'
2 bedrooms, 1 bath
basement, crawl space, or slab foundation,
please specify when ordering

The Provider II cabin is the perfect rustic design for a woodside getaway. The cabin's L-shaped kitchen with convenient pantry is adjacent to the dining area for easy mealtimes and cleanup. This cabin also has easy access to the laundry, linen, and storage closets. Both of the bedrooms also include ample closet space for keeping everything organized. From the moment you enter, you will call this place home!

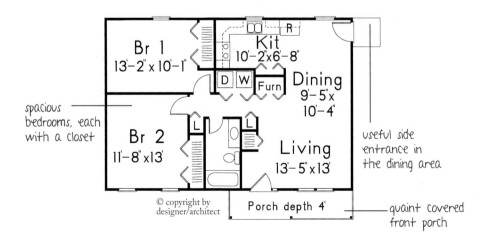

spacious bedrooms, each with a closet

Br 1
13'-2" x 10'-1"

Kit
10'-2"x6-8"

Dining
9'-5"x
10'-4"

Br 2
11'-8"x13'

Living
13'-5"x13'

useful side entrance in the dining area

© copyright by designer/architect

Porch depth 4'

quaint covered front porch

ENCANTADA LOG CABIN

The Encantada log cabin has rugged mountain good looks with plenty of opportunities for catching a beautiful view through the numerous windows. A corner fireplace in the great room coupled with a two-story ceiling adds a touch of class to this rustic cabin. Wonderful French doors lead out to the deck, perfect for outdoor entertaining. The kitchen has a eating bar for enjoying meals.

PLAN #C19-088D-0027

1040 square feet of living area
width: 24' depth: 30'
1 bedroom, 1 bath
log exterior walls
crawl space foundation

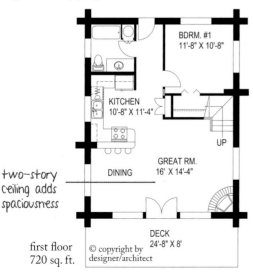

two-story ceiling adds spaciousness

first floor
720 sq. ft.

© copyright by designer/architect

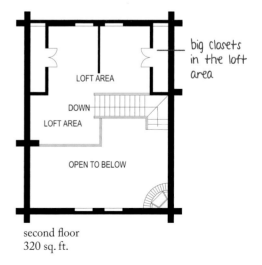

big closets in the loft area

second floor
320 sq. ft.

WOODSMILL CABIN

PLAN #C19-007D-0042

914 square feet of living area
width: 30'   depth: 33'
2 bedrooms, 1 bath
basement foundation

Perfect for a sloping hillside waterfront lot, the Woodsmill cabin offers a quaint and comfortable dwelling with a living room that includes a cozy fireplace. The dining area has a sunny bay window, an open staircase, and a pass-through style kitchen creating an open interior throughout, while the lower level includes generous garage space and a finished laundry and mechanical room.

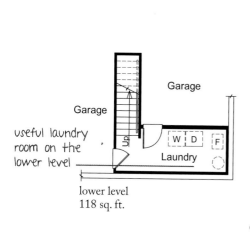

useful laundry room on the lower level

lower level
118 sq. ft.

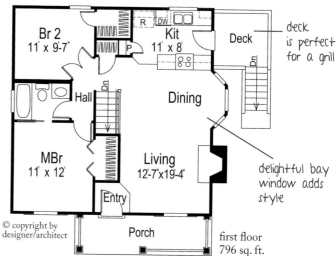

deck is perfect for a grill

delightful bay window adds style

first floor
796 sq. ft.

Br 2
11' x 9'-7"

Kit
11' x 8'

Deck

Hall

Dining

MBr
11' x 12'

Living
12'-7"x19'-4"

Entry

Porch

© copyright by designer/architect

LANAWOOD CABIN

The Lanawood cabin home features a spacious living room that connects to the efficiently designed kitchen with a convenient raised snack bar. The lovely kitchen and bedroom both access the rear porch as well as the covered or screened porch, offering exceptional outdoor living comfort whatever time of day or season. A handy bonus room can be utilized as a hobby room or second bedroom.

PLAN #C19-077D-0008

600 square feet of living area
width: 31'-8"   depth: 26'
1 bedroom, 1 bath
basement, crawl space, or slab foundation, please specify when ordering

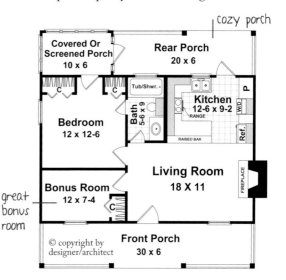

cozy porch

great bonus room

Covered Or Screened Porch
10 x 6

Rear Porch
20 x 6

Tub/Shwr.

Kitchen
12-6 x 9-2

RANGE

W/D

P

Ref.

Bedroom
12 x 12-6

Bath
5-6 x 9

RAISED BAR

Living Room
18 X 11

FIREPLACE

Bonus Room
12 x 7-4

C

Front Porch
30 x 6

© copyright by designer/architect

EDGEBRIAR CABIN

PLAN #C19-002D-7531

720 square feet of living area
width: 24' depth: 30'
2 bedrooms, 1 bath
crawl space or slab foundation,
please specify when ordering
material list included

The Edgebriar cabin has an uncomplicated design that stands the test of time. Always a crowd pleaser, the deep covered front porch really creates the added outdoor space people crave. Whether reading in the shade or chatting with family and friends, this no doubt will be a favorite spot to unwind. The U-shaped kitchen is high function and overlooks the living area. Two bedrooms are placed in the back of the home near a laundry closet and full bathroom.

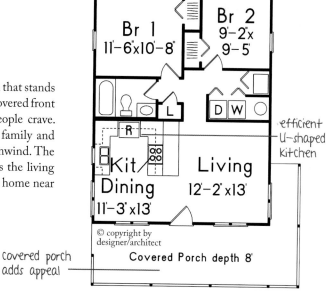

Br 1
11'-6"x10'-8"

Br 2
9'-2"x 9'-5"

efficient U-shaped kitchen

Kit/ Dining
11'-3'x13'

Living
12'-2'x13'

© copyright by designer/architect

covered porch adds appeal

Covered Porch depth 8'

COZY RETREAT CABIN

Ideal for a shallow lot, the Cozy Retreat cabin is the perfect escape on a long weekend. Step into the combined kitchen, dining, and living areas that share a vaulted ceiling for added openness and discover a place you will love coming back to time and time again. The cozy fireplace lures you to stay awhile and relax. The vaulted ceiling continues into a bedroom that features a walk-in closet. When it's time to kick back after dinner, there's no better place than the screened porch.

PLAN #C19-055D-0943

828 square feet of living area
width: 58'   depth: 18'
1 bedroom, 1 bath
crawl space or slab foundation,
please specify when ordering

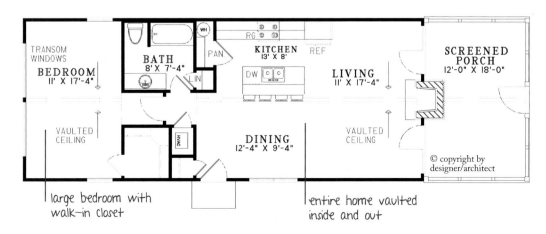

large bedroom with
walk-in closet

entire home vaulted
inside and out

PINEHURST I CABIN

PLAN #C19-001D-0081

1160 square feet of living area
width: 44'   depth: 28'
3 bedrooms, 1 1/2 baths
crawl space or slab foundation,
please specify when ordering

The Pinehurst I cabin has combined dining and great rooms creating that open living atmosphere everyone is drawn to. The dining room has outdoor access, perfect for a grill. The U-shaped kitchen includes a breakfast bar and a convenient laundry closet. The master bedroom features a private half bath and a large closet. There are also two other bedrooms, both with ample closet space.

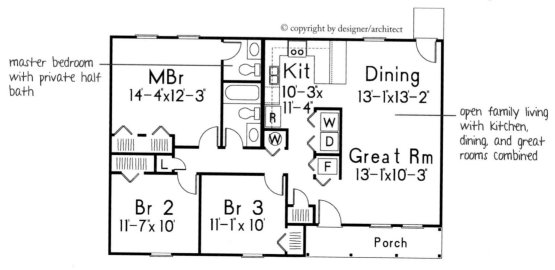

master bedroom with private half bath

open family living with kitchen, dining, and great rooms combined

© copyright by designer/architect

MBr 14'-4"x12'-3"

Kit 10'-3"x 11'-4"

Dining 13'-1"x13'-2"

Great Rm 13'-1"x10'-3"

Br 2 11'-7"x 10'

Br 3 11'-1"x 10'

Porch

SCENIC HILL
Take time out at the Scenic Hill cabin and enjoy a covered front porch for story-telling at night as well as a vaulted open interior. The kitchen will be a hub of activity with its eating bar. Twin bedrooms provide a place to rest your head, and both have a closet.

PLAN #C19-141D-0218
1000 square feet of living area
width: 36'-6"   depth: 34'
2 bedrooms, 1 bath
crawl space or slab foundation,
please specify when ordering

BOWMAN
The Bowman country cabin has a cathedral ceiling adding spaciousness, and a stone fireplace creating warmth. A large dining room extends off the kitchen and remains open. The master bedroom is located near the main living areas for maximum convenience.

PLAN #C19-020D-0015
1191 square feet of living area
width: 44'-6"   depth: 59'
3 bedrooms, 2 baths
slab foundation standard;
basement or crawl space available for a fee

ELFIN COVE
The Elfin Cove log cabin is defined by its large covered front porch and screened porch adding great outdoor living spaces. A cozy and comfortable interior includes a living room with a kitchen/dining room.

PLAN #C19-073D-0023
1122 square feet of living area
width: 35'   depth: 39'
3 bedrooms, 2 baths
crawl space foundation standard;
basement or daylight basement available for a fee

HUNTER'S COVE
After hunting or fishing, this is the place to relax. The covered porch is ideal for gathering and swapping stories from the day, or retire to one of two bedrooms at night's end.

PLAN #C19-002D-7508
576 square feet of living area
width: 24'   depth: 24'
2 bedrooms, 1 bath
pier foundation
material list included

DOGWOOD
The Dogwood cabin has a full-length front covered porch creating the perfect spot to enjoy the outdoors. Combined dining and living areas create an open feel inside. A see-through fireplace between the bedroom and living area adds character and warmth.

PLAN #C19-058D-0010
676 square feet of living area
width: 26' depth: 32'
1 bedroom, 1 bath
crawl space foundation

REMINGTON COVE
The Remington Cove cabin is an ideal lakeside escape. Enter to an open floor plan with an eat-in kitchen and bayed family room sharing a cozy two-sided fireplace. A laundry closet is conveniently near the secondary bedroom.

PLAN #C19-032D-0357
874 square feet of living area
width: 36' depth: 24'
2 bedrooms, 1 bath
2" x 6" exterior walls
crawl space standard;
monolithic slab or floating slab available for a fee

Blueprint PRICING and ORDERING + VISIT houseplansandmore.com + 1-800-373-2646

CARLO
The Carlo modern cabin promises efficiency and cutting-edge style. A covered porch provides a place to rest, and the inside has one space with a kitchen. A space-saving pocket door creates privacy for the bedroom.

PLAN #C19-126D-1148
396 square feet of living area
width: 22' depth: 18'
1 bedroom, 1 bath
2" x 6" exterior walls
pilings foundation

MAYBERRY COVE
The Mayberry Cove cabin has a rustic porch. An open floor plan prevails in this cozy cabin. There is plenty of space for preparing meals in the kitchen, and a sitting area doubles as sleeping space.

PLAN #C19-058D-0014
416 square feet of living area
width: 26' depth: 22'
1 sleeping/sitting area, 1 bath
footing and foundation wall

SENECA PEAK
The Seneca Peak cabin has a covered porch opening to a vaulted family room warmed by a cozy fireplace. An eating bar creates extra space at mealtimes. Two bedrooms sit privately on opposing sides with a central bath for convenience.

PLAN #C19-058D-0029
1000 square feet of living area
width: 42'   depth: 34'
2 bedrooms, 1 bath
crawl space foundation

DILLON
Don't let this tiny modern cabin fool you, the Dillon cabin feels spacious with its slanted ceiling inside creating added space. Walk into a living area with the kitchen around the corner. The two bedrooms are on opposite sides for added privacy.

PLAN #C19-126D-1149
528 square feet of living area
width: 24'   depth: 22'
2 bedrooms, 1 bath
2" x 6" exterior walls
pilings foundation

MIKA
Whether the Mika modern cabin is built as an in-law suite, or as a stylish retreat, you will love that every inch is maximized for comfort. Front and back covered porches are great additions to the open interior layout.

PLAN #C19-126D-1152
599 square feet of living area
width: 38'   depth: 18'
1 bedroom, 1 bath
2" x 6" exterior walls
pier foundation

HILLTOP GREEN
The Hilltop Green cabin has one-of-a-kind modern style. A spiral staircase ascends to a loft overlooking the vaulted great room. The kitchen has a built-in eating bar with great room views.

PLAN #C19-080D-0015
840 square feet of living area
width: 20'   depth: 28'
1 bedroom, 1 bath
2" x 6" exterior walls
walk-out basement or basement foundation,
please specify when ordering

APRIL KNOLL

This cozy cottage offers many comforts of home, including a vaulted great room, washer and dryer closet, and a U-shaped kitchen that opens onto the rear screened porch. Accessible via a ladder is a vaulted loft that overlooks the living room.

PLAN #C19-077D-0286
1016 square feet of living area
width: 30' depth: 36'
2 bedrooms, 1 bath
crawl space foundation standard;
slab available for a fee

RUSTY RIDGE

The open floor plan is fantastic in this Craftsman style home. The foyer includes plenty of closet space. The washer and dryer are located on the first floor, and the second floor consists of two bedrooms with large closets plus a full bathroom.

PLAN #C19-032D-0808
900 square feet of living area
width: 32' depth: 24'
2 bedrooms, 11/2 baths
basement foundation standard; crawl space,
floating slab, or monolithic slab available for a fee

HARMONY BLUFF

The Harmony Bluff rustic cabin is topped with a soaring vaulted ceiling. The kitchen looks out over the great room with fireplace, and twin bedrooms provide comfort and privacy.

PLAN #C19-141D-0077
1000 square feet of living area
width: 27' depth: 46'
2 bedrooms, 1 bath
slab foundation

CHAPPELOW HILL

This country cabin would be a great in-law suite with its large bathroom with utility room and walk-in shower. A living room, nearby kitchen, and master bedroom complete the home.

PLAN #C19-141D-0230
676 square feet of living area
width: 26' depth: 26'
1 bedroom, 1 bath
slab or crawl space foundation,
please specify when ordering

LIVING LARGE IN A SMALL HOME

Out with the old and in with the new. Gone are the days of excessively large and wasteful mansions. Now, small homes rule the market. They cost less to maintain, they are easier to clean, they bring family closer together, and the taxes are far lower.

With so many benefits, it's no wonder that many families are making the switch to more modestly sized abodes. However, it's important to remember the cost — less space! This means that you must maintain optimal use of your available space, clear out the clutter, and plan out everything. No more impulse buys because they simply won't fit into your smaller place!

FLOOR PLAN

Consider every room carefully and evaluate your needs. For the smaller home, an open floor plan with fewer interior walls opens up your available space and creates the illusion of even more space since pesky walls aren't obstructing the view. High ceilings also open up the home for relatively low cost and they help reduce feelings of claustrophobia and restriction. Additionally, certain rooms such as formal dining and living rooms have outlived their usefulness. Only utilized a handful of times a year, converting these outdated rooms into multipurpose spaces or offices is certainly a viable option.

DOORS AND WINDOWS

Doors are another feature to consider in your small home. With limited space, every little bit counts, and installing trendy barn-style or pocket doors instead of hinge doors can free up an average of 10 square feet. That's a lot of space that you can put to good use!

Other ways to create the impression of space include adding large windows into your design or even a skylight. These windows filter in more natural light, brightening and reinforcing the feeling of spaciousness in the interior.

STORAGE

Once you have the floor plan figured out, it's time to think about a very important matter: storage. Over our lifetimes we accumulate stuff. Whether it's useful or full of memories, we need places to put our knickknacks, and with less space, organization and creativity play key roles. However, no matter how organized you are, if there is no room, there is simply no room.

So if you're downsizing, or trying to get your smaller home in order, remember that you may need to assess all of your belongings before picking nonessentials to throw out.

Now that you're left with essentials and anything that you can't bear to part with, it's time to consider alternative storage options. Built-in shelves, for example, free up a lot of floor space and create a more open atmosphere. Also, wall hooks, floor-to-ceiling shelving, and storage under the stairs or bed can clean up the disorder of everyday life. It is important to remember that open shelving, as opposed to closed cabinets, creates a more open feel and the illusion of more space. And, don't forget to utilize your full vertical storage capacity! Oftentimes we neglect to fill up the available vertical space and just try to cram everything in at eye level or below. You may need to keep a footstool nearby, but the added storage space is well worth it.

COLOR

When you're painting your small house, just remember that dark colors create an intimate, cozy feeling whereas lighter hues open up a room. So, depending upon how you want to feel, you may want a nice and cozy, darker home, or you may want an open and fresh, lighter home. You may even want a mix of dark and light rooms. In creating an effective light color scheme, it is important to choose pale, soft paint colors for your walls and then use your furniture to create the colored accents. Stick to plain solid colored furniture because it will keep your small room from looking cluttered by bold prints and patterns.

DECORATION AND FURNITURE

It's time to decorate your home, but you don't want to waste space on flashy, useless decorations. Instead, keep the displayed knickknacks to a minimum to reduce the visual clutter and give a more airy feel to your home. Without all of the odds and ends closing in on your visual field, you're free to appreciate the items that are on display without feeling crowded out. Also, hanging mirrors on your walls will give the illusion of more space and provide an attractive wall embellishment at the same time.

Furnishing your small space can be both exciting and challenging. Not everything will fit well, so remember to plan out your furniture. Instead of choosing a myriad of smaller furnishings, pick out several larger pieces to create a focal point in the room and avoid the muddled, chaotic feel of too much small furniture. Also, be sure to consider the multi-purpose potential of your furniture. Ottomans and chests can double as storage or coffee tables. Let your creativity reign and you will give your house a unique, yet functional interior perfect for living large in a small home!

COTTAGES

Plan #C19-032D-0358 is found on page 71.

While cabins evoke a sense of all things rustic, cottages shift toward a charming, nostalgic country feel. Like their rustic counterpart, cottages are small in size, but packed with personality. Cottages steer clear of a cabin's usually rustic exterior and are often adorned with pastel colors and intricate trimwork that borderlines Victorian style. Cottages are especially popular near the water, both coastal and lakeside, and can create the ideal getaway home or investment property. Whatever your specific need, you will fall in love with the undeniable charm these cottages provide.

ROBBIN COTTAGE

Live life like a fairytale in the European-inspired, quaint Robbin cottage. With attention to detail at every turn, cottage life is definitely not primitive in this luxurious cottage that boasts an amenity-packed kitchen, an open floor plan, vaulted living area, and homeowner quarters that are comfortable and bright. Don't let size fool you; this cottage is designed to pamper and provides a luxury environment to prove it.

© copyright by designer/architect

VAULTED
MASTER
14'/2" X 10'/8" +/-

BLT-IN

VAULTED
BR. 2
10'/8" X 11'/2"

BLT-IN PAN

W/D

washer and dryer space in the bathroom

large coat closet and pantry combo

PORCH

VAULTED
LIVING
12' X 15'/8" +

(8' CLG)

PLAN #C19-011D-0313

782 square feet of living area
width: 24'   depth: 44'
2 bedrooms, 1 bath
2" x 6" exterior walls
joisted crawl space or post & beam foundation
standard; slab or basement available for a fee

McPHERSON COTTAGE

The McPherson Victorian cottage has a striking turret and covered gazebo-shaped front porch creating excellent curb appeal. The bay window brightens the living room, and a corner fireplace invites guests into this charming space and begs them to relax and stay awhile. Handy double pocket doors separate the living room from the dining area, while also allowing no wasted space. A rounded snack bar connects the kitchen to the dining room and includes seating for three people. Inside and out, this cottage is a star!

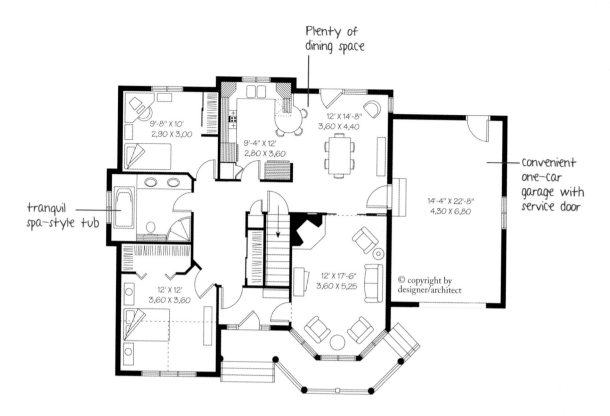

Plenty of
dining space

9'-8" X 10'
2,90 X 3,00

9'-4" X 12'
2,80 X 3,60

12' X 14'-8"
3,60 X 4,40

convenient
one-car
garage with
service door

tranquil
spa-style tub

14'-4" X 22'-8"
4,30 X 6,80

© copyright by
designer/architect

12' X 12'
3,60 X 3,60

12' X 17'-6"
3,60 X 5,25

PLAN #C19-032D-0139

1191 square feet of living area
width: 50'   depth: 36'
2 bedrooms, 1 bath
2" x 6" exterior walls
basement foundation standard; crawl space,
monolithic slab, or floating slab available for a fee

BELLE COVE COTTAGE

Elegantly European, the Belle Cove cottage mimics the style of a French Chateau, but on a much smaller scale. This design perfects the open layout without a hitch. Two bedrooms, each with their own bath, create privacy and everyday comfort for guests or a live-in parent. The central hub is the kitchen where all activity will radiate from. Dining and living areas effectively merge, forming a larger area. And there's even a one-car garage.

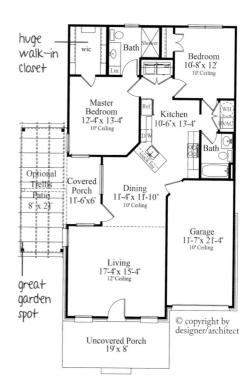

huge walk-in closet

wic

Bath

Shower

Bedroom
10'-8" x 12'
10' Ceiling

Master Bedroom
12'-4" x 13'-4"
10' Ceiling

Lin.

Ref.

Kitchen
10'-6" x 13'-4"

WH

HVAC

Bath

D/W

Stack Bar

Optional Trellis Patio
8' x 22'

Covered Porch
11'-6" x 6'

Dining
11'-4" x 11'-10"
10' Ceiling

Garage
11'-7" x 21'-4"
10' Ceiling

great garden spot

Living
17'-4" x 15'-4"
12' Ceiling

© copyright by designer/architect

Uncovered Porch
19' x 8'

PLAN #C19-084D-0052

1170 square feet of living area
width: 38'-6"   depth: 48'-6"
2 bedrooms, 2 baths
slab foundation standard;
crawl space or basement available for a fee

DIGBY COTTAGE

The Digby cottage is a fantasy come true! Have you ever seen such a stylish, quaint dwelling? Its rustic appeal and attention to detail begs you to knock on the door and invite yourself in. Designed as guest quarters, this cottage has a cozy corner fireplace for added ambiance. The kitchenette is efficient and offers basic amenities. A spacious walk-in closet provides more than ample storage. The bathroom has a walk-in shower, great for people of all ages and abilities. This cottage is what dreams are made of!

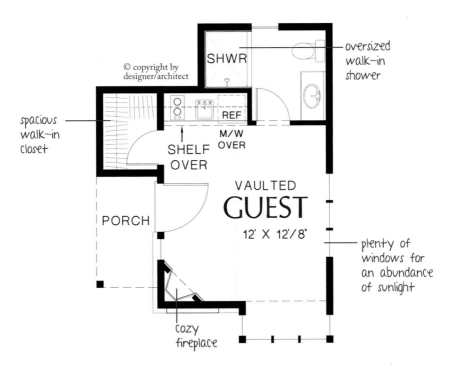

SHWR

oversized walk-in shower

spacious walk-in closet

REF

M/W OVER

SHELF OVER

VAULTED
GUEST
12' X 12'/8'

PORCH

plenty of windows for an abundance of sunlight

cozy fireplace

PLAN #C19-011D-0431

300 square feet of living area
width: 17'-6"   depth: 23'
1 bath
2" x 6" exterior walls
slab foundation

MILFORD COVE COTTAGE

The Milford Cove cottage has an alluring Palladian-style window gracing its exterior, while it also floods the living room with added sunlight. The incredible dining room flows into a kitchen that offers a dual sink, handsome cabinetry, and loads of counterspace. The master suite is simply luxurious with bright windows, a walk-in closet, and a separate shower for the ultimate in relaxation. The second floor has two bedrooms and a full bath, which can easily accommodate a family.

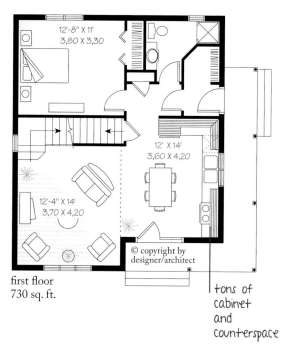

12'-8" X 11'
3,80 X 3,30

12' X 14'
3,60 X 4,20

12'-4" 14'
3,70 X 4,20

© copyright by
designer/architect

first floor
730 sq. ft.

tons of
cabinet
and
counterspace

14'-4" X 11'
4,30 X 3,30

10'-10" X 11'
3,25 X 3,30

second floor
438 sq. ft.

loft-style
bedroom

PLAN #C19-032D-0554

1168 square feet of living area
width: 25'-8"   depth: 30'
3 bedrooms, 2 baths
2" x 6" exterior walls
basement foundation standard; crawl space,
monolithic slab, or floating slab available for a fee

BALDWIN LANE COTTAGE

The Baldwin Lane cottage has an ever-so-famous wraparound porch just waiting for you to enjoy. This two-story design embraces an open atmosphere on the first floor, making it a fun floor plan when entertaining. The second floor is where you can retreat after a busy day. Both bedrooms can be found there, and each are vaulted and share a sizable bathroom. Don't let the undeniable charm and comfort of the Baldwin Lane cottage pass you by.

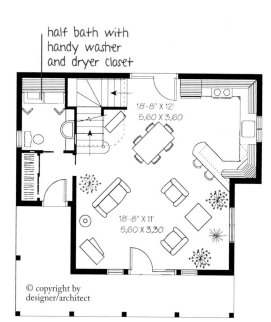

half bath with handy washer and dryer closet

18'-8" X 12'
5,60 X 3,60

18'-8" X 11'
5,60 X 3,30

© copyright by designer/architect

first floor
630 sq. ft.

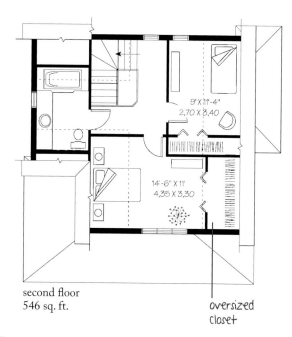

9' X 11'-4"
2,70 X 3,40

14'-6" X 11'
4,35 X 3,30

second floor
546 sq. ft.

oversized closet

PLAN #C19-032D-0889

1176 square feet of living area
width: 30'   depth: 24'
2 bedrooms, 1½ baths
2" x 6" exterior walls
basement foundation standard; crawl space, floating slab, or monolithic slab available for a fee

LYNDALE COTTAGE

Simple yet beautiful Craftsman-style windows bring interest to the exterior of the cheerful Lyndale Cottage. The comfortable covered front porch is the perfect place to sit back, enjoy the outdoors, and wave to the neighbors. The lovely kitchen is cozy yet highly functional. The romantic master suite is privately located on the second floor and contains a large window in the bedroom, as well as a private bathroom with a double-bowl vanity. Practical, functional, and graced with Craftsman style, this cottage is refreshing yet timeless at the same time.

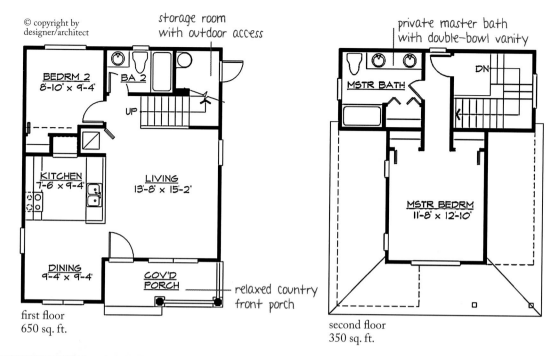

storage room
with outdoor access

private master bath
with double-bowl vanity

© copyright by
designer/architect

BEDRM 2
8'-10" x 9-4"

BA 2

UP

KITCHEN
7'-6" x 9-4"

LIVING
13'-8" x 15-2"

DINING
9'-4" x 9'-4"

COV'D PORCH

relaxed country
front porch

first floor
650 sq. ft.

MSTR BATH

DN

MSTR BEDRM
11'-8" x 12'-10"

second floor
350 sq. ft.

PLAN #C19-071D-0013

1000 square feet of living area
width: 24'   depth: 30'
2 bedrooms, 2 baths
2" x 6" exterior walls
crawl space foundation

AVONDALE LANE COTTAGE

The Avondale Lane cottage has a friendly and welcoming feel the minute you lay your eyes on it. Its charming covered porch will put a smile on your face. Inside, the living room is vaulted and remains separate from a kitchen with enough space for dining. The bedroom is generous in size and has two closets for keeping things tidy. A bathroom is placed in a convenient location. Living will be easy in this lovely little cottage.

Bath
8' × 10'-8"

Kitchen
10' × 10'-8"

kitchen has space for a dining table

Closet
6'-4" × 3'

Closet
6'-4" × 2'

Living Room
13'-8" × 10'-4"

Bedroom
10'-4" × 10'-7"

Porch
11'-10" × 4'-10"

cozy covered porch

WD

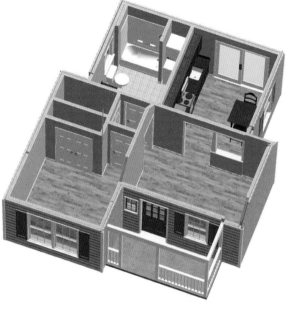

PLAN #C19-156D-0006

550 square feet of living area
width: 25'   depth: 28'
1 bedroom, 1 bath
slab foundation standard;
crawl space available for a fee

FAIRHAVEN HILL COTTAGE

Life in the Fairhaven Hill cottage will be bliss! Besides its abundance of exterior charm, this tiny home has the most cheerful interior. Walls of windows emit tons of natural sunlight, creating an interior you'll be excited to decorate. An expansive L-shaped kitchen flows seamlessly into the living area. The bedroom has direct access into the bathroom. Whether this is a vacation cottage or a permanent dwelling, this cottage is truly something special.

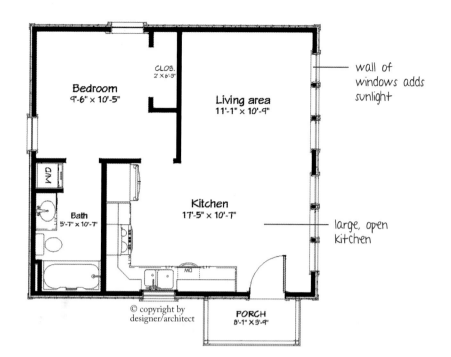

Bedroom
9'-6" × 10'-5"

CLOS.
2' × 6'-3"

Living area
11'-1" × 10'-9"

wall of
windows adds
sunlight

W/D

Bath
5'-7" × 10'-7"

Kitchen
17'-5" × 10'-7"

large, open
kitchen

DW

© copyright by
designer/architect

PORCH
8'-1" X 3'-9"

PLAN #C19-156D-0007

528 square feet of living area
width: 24'   depth: 26'
1 bedroom, 1 bath
slab foundation standard;
crawl space available for a fee

EXETER CREEK COTTAGE

The front covered porch of the Exeter Creek cottage offers an ideal outdoor living area, perfect for those beautiful spring evenings when the birds are chirping. A snack bar counter in the kitchen creates a quick and easy dining area near the great room. The large laundry area accesses the outdoors as well as the kitchen for added convenience to the backyard. Two ample-sized bedrooms enjoy their own closets and a nearby full bath. Sneak away to the Exeter Creek cottage and create lasting memories!

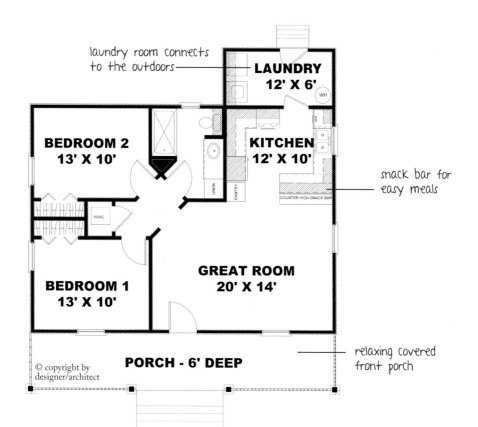

laundry room connects
to the outdoors

LAUNDRY
12' X 6'

WH

BEDROOM 2
13' X 10'

KITCHEN
12' X 10'

snack bar for
easy meals

LINEN

PANTRY

COUNTER HIGH SNACK BAR

HVAC

BEDROOM 1
13' X 10'

GREAT ROOM
20' X 14'

© copyright by
designer/architect

PORCH - 6' DEEP

relaxing covered
front porch

PLAN #C19-028D-0001

864 square feet of living area
width: 33'   depth: 36'
2 bedrooms, 1 bath
crawl space or slab foundation,
please specify when ordering

CANTON CREST COTTAGE

The Canton Crest cottage has covered front and rear porches with ceiling fans, keeping you comfortable in balmy weather. A dramatic vaulted ceiling crowns the family room and kitchen, creating a truly effective openness. Two generously sized bedrooms, each with a walk-in closet, share a bathroom.

PLAN #C19-013D-0154

953 square feet of living area
width: 36'   depth: 42'-4"
2 bedrooms, 1½ baths
crawl space foundation standard;
basement or slab available for a fee

both bedrooms have direct access to the bathroom

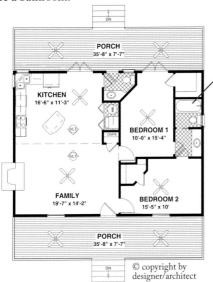

PORCH
35'-8" x 7'-7"

KITCHEN
16'-6" x 11'-3"

BEDROOM 1
10'-0" x 15'-4"

COATS

VLT

FAMILY
19'-7" x 14'-2"

BEDROOM 2
15'-5" x 10'

PORCH
35'-8" x 7'-7"

DN

© copyright by designer/architect

SUMMERLEDGE COTTAGE

PLAN #C19-007D-0128

1072 square feet of living area
345 bonus square feet
width: 52'   depth: 40'-8"
2 bedrooms, 2 baths
walk-out basement foundation

The Summerledge cottage integrates open and screened front porches, guaranteeing comfortable summer enjoyment. An oversized garage includes a shop and storage. The U-shaped kitchen and breakfast area are adjacent to a vaulted living room with patio access through sliding glass doors. Optional living space, including a third bedroom and a bath, can be found on the lower level.

flexibility to increase square footage

Br 3
13-4'x12-3'

Basement

D W

Basement

L

Hall

optional lower level 345 sq. ft.

MBr
11-7'x15-6'

Br 2
10' x 12-11"

Shop

Hall

L R

Garage
21-8' x 26-4'

Kit
9-7' x 9'

P

DW

© copyright by designer/architect

Patio

Living
14' x 18-9'

Brk fst
10-9' x 9'

Screened Porch
18-4' x 13'

breezy screened porch for outdoor enjoyment

first floor
1072 sq. ft.

E

Porch

DANBURY HOLLOW COTTAGE

The Danbury Hollow cottage has a refined cottage feel that just oozes charm. It is also the perfect size for a small or narrow lot. The angled kitchen is intriguing to the eye and contains lots of counter space for easily prepping daily meals. One open living space creates an enjoyable environment for entertaining or relaxation. Two sizable bedrooms skillfully share a bath with a large whirlpool tub.

PLAN #C19-032D-0116

946 square feet of living area
width: 30'   depth: 35'
2 bedrooms, 1 bath
2" x 6" exterior walls
basement foundation standard;
crawl space, monolithic slab, or floating slab
available for a fee

open
floor
plan

18' X 12'
5,40 X 3,60

10'-4" X 9'-6"
3,10 X 2,85

13' X 15'
3,90 X 4,50

13' X 11'
3,90 X 3,30

© copyright by
designer/architect

Blueprint PRICING and ORDERING + VISIT houseplansandmore.com + 1-800-373-2646

WILDBROOK LAKE COTTAGE

PLAN #C19-032D-0358

1148 square feet of living area
width: 28'   depth: 26'
1 bedroom, 1½ baths
2" x 6" exterior walls
basement foundation standard;
crawl space, monolithic slab, or floating slab
available for a fee

The Wildbrook Lake cottage is completely open for a bright atmosphere. The kitchen includes a unique island with seating for quick meals or space to serve buffet-style. The half bath on the first floor has space for a washer and dryer. French doors lead to the majestic second floor master bedroom that enjoys a huge walk-in closet and a private bath with a separate whirlpool tub and corner shower.

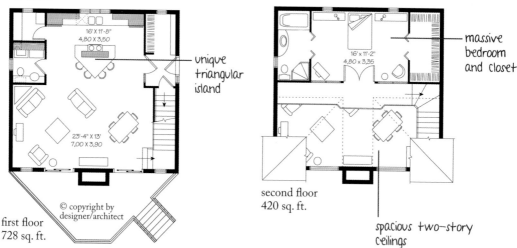

unique triangular island

16' X 11'-8"
4,80 X 3,50

23'-4" X 13'
7,00 X 3,90

© copyright by designer/architect

first floor
728 sq. ft.

massive bedroom and closet

16' x 11'-2"
4,80 x 3,35

second floor
420 sq. ft.

spacious two-story ceilings

HAVERHILL COTTAGE

The vaulted ceiling in the family room of the Haverhill cottage will create quite a stir. The covered entry porch provides plenty of shade on warm, summer evenings. The open L-shaped kitchen has a functional layout. The convenient laundry room is located near the rear entry and bedroom #1. Bedroom #2 on the second floor is a great space for a home office or guest room.

PLAN #C19-040D-0028

828 square feet of living area
width: 28'   depth: 31'-6"
2 bedrooms, 1 bath
crawl space foundation

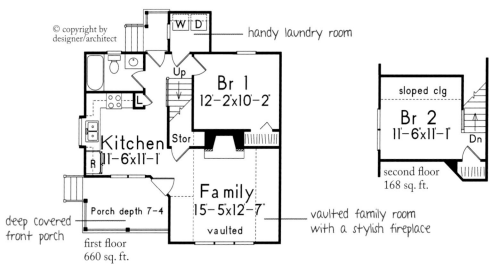

© copyright by designer/architect

handy laundry room

W D

Up

Br 1
12-2"x10-2"

Kitchen
11-6"x11-1"

Stor

R

L

deep covered front porch

Porch depth 7-4

Family
15-5"x12-7"
vaulted

first floor
660 sq. ft.

vaulted family room with a stylish fireplace

sloped clg

Br 2
11-6"x11-1"

Dn

second floor
168 sq. ft.

SUMMERSMILL COTTAGE

PLAN #C19-007D-0135

801 square feet of living area
width: 57'   depth: 36'-4"
2 bedrooms, 1 bath
slab foundation

A wraparound porch, roof dormer, and fancy stonework all contribute to the delightful and charming exterior of the Summersmill cottage. A vaulted living room enjoys a stone fireplace and lots of windows. The well-equipped kitchen has a snack bar and bayed dining area with access to a rear patio. Two bedrooms with a bath and a large workshop in the garage for the family handyman are great extras in this small floor plan.

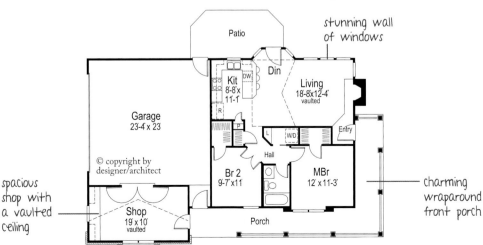

FAIR VIEW COTTAGE

The Fair View cottage offers all of the things cottage living is about. Abundant charm, Southern-style covered front and side porches, and a welcoming floor plan. The family room with fireplace greets all those who come through the front door. A bay-shaped kitchen with island is ready for any task at hand and can easily reach a grill on the deck. Life's simple pleasures will be enjoyed to the fullest in this darling home.

PLAN #C19-139D-0001

1068 square feet of living area
width: 39'-7"   depth: 51'-9"
2 bedrooms, 1 bath
2" x 6" exterior walls
crawl space foundation standard;
basement or slab available for a fee

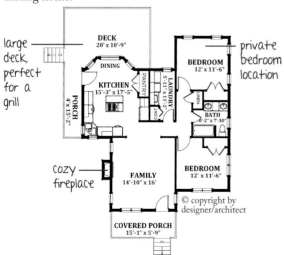

large deck, perfect for a grill

DECK
20' x 10'-9"

DINING

KITCHEN
15'-3" x 17'-5"

PANTRY

LAUNDRY
5'-11" x 11'-2"

PORCH
4' x 15'-2"

BEDROOM
12' x 11'-6"

private bedroom location

LINEN

BATH
8'-2" x 7'-10"

cozy fireplace

FAMILY
14'-10" x 16'

BEDROOM
12' x 11'-6"

© copyright by designer/architect

COVERED PORCH
15'-1" x 5'-9"

FOXLAND COTTAGE

PLAN #C19-045D-0017

954 square feet of living area
width: 25'-8"   depth: 30'
3 bedrooms, 2 baths
basement foundation

Step from the shaded covered front porch inside this charming cottage and find a convenient coat closet near the front entry. The kitchen has a cozy bayed eating area. The great room has access to both the front and back porches. The master bedroom has a walk-in closet and private bath. The second floor is comprised of two bedrooms and a full bath centered between them for convenience. Charm and function are equally achieved in this friendly cottage!

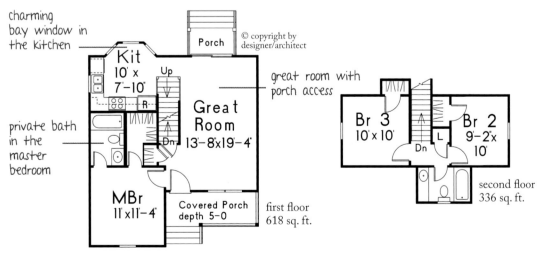

charming bay window in the kitchen

private bath in the master bedroom

Porch

© copyright by designer/architect

Kit
10' x 7'-10"

Up

R

Great Room
13'-8"x19'-4"

Dn

great room with porch access

MBr
11'x11'-4"

Covered Porch
depth 5-0

first floor
618 sq. ft.

Br 3
10' x 10'

Br 2
9'-2"x 10'

Dn

L

second floor
336 sq. ft.

SHAKER LANE COTTAGE

Timeless Colonial charm has been perfected in the Shaker Lane cottage. Covered front and back porches truly make this home, while spilling living into the outdoors in a seamless way. The great room has a fireplace as a focal point and the bedroom and bath have a nearby washer and dryer closet.

PLAN #C19-011D-0316

960 square feet of living area
width: 30'   depth: 48'
1 bedroom, 1 bath
2" x 6" exterior walls
joisted crawl space foundation standard;
slab or basement available for a fee

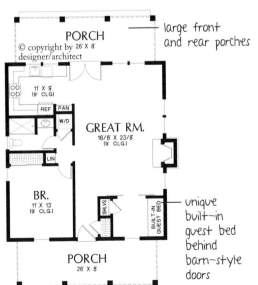

PORCH
© copyright by 26' X 8'
designer/architect

large front and rear porches

11 X 9'
(9' CLG.)

REF PAN

W/D

GREAT RM.
16/8' X 23/8'
(9' CLG.)

LIN

BR.
11 X 13'
(9' CLG.)

SHLVS

BUILT-IN GUEST BED

PORCH
26' X 8'

unique built-in guest bed behind barn-style doors

OLSON LANE COTTAGE

PLAN #C19-051D-0847

1047 square feet of living area
width: 40'   depth: 46'
2 bedrooms, 1 bath
2" x 6" exterior walls
basement foundation standard;
crawl space or slab available for a fee

The Olson Lane Craftsman cottage has tremendous curb appeal with its spacious covered front porch offering additional outdoor living space. The open-concept floor plan has the kitchen, dining, and great room blended together, creating a more spacious living area. The bedrooms are located to the left of the home behind the garage for privacy.

open vaulted living space

DECK

MBR.
9'-1 1/8" CEILING
15'8"x13'

KIT.
VAULTED CEILING
9'x9'6"

DIN. RM.
VAULTED CEILING
8'6"x9'6"

BR. #2
9'-1 1/8" CEILING
11'8"x10'6"

GRT. RM.
VAULTED CEILING
17'6"x14'6"

E.
CATHEDRAL
CEILING

2 CAR GARAGE
20'4"x20'8"

© copyright by
designer/architect

high ceiling for openness

DuPREE
The DuPree cottage has gathering space highlighted by a warm fireplace. Box windows brighten the kitchen, while a window wall and a door flood the dining area with sunlight. A luxurious bath has a corner whirlpool tub and the home has 2" x 6" exterior walls.

PLAN #C19-032D-0390
1072 square feet of living area
231 bonus square feet
width: 32' depth: 42'
2 bedrooms, 1 bath
basement foundation standard;
crawl space or floating slab available for a fee

COVENTRY CIRCLE
The Coventry Circle cottage is the ideal starter or retirement home. The family room is designed for gatherings and is open to a dining area. The kitchen has a handy lunch counter for quick meals and accesses a patio, perfect for grilling.

PLAN #C19-032D-0088
1098 square feet of living area
width: 32' depth: 36'-8"
2 bedrooms, 1 bath
2" x 6" exterior walls
basement foundation

GLENWOODS
Triple windows on two walls of the living room brightens the Glenwoods cottage beyond belief. An open kitchen and spacious bedroom complete this stylish and sensible cottage design.

PLAN #C19-156D-0002
576 square feet of living area
width: 24' depth: 27'-6"
1 bedroom, 1 bath
slab foundation standard;
crawl space available for a fee

WALSH
Sloped ceilings in the living room and bedroom grace the interior of the Walsh cottage. Covered front and back porches add charm and outdoor enjoyment, while the kitchen has a handy island near the dinette.

PLAN #C19-130D-0361
550 square feet of living area
width: 21'-8" depth: 35'
1 bedroom, 1 bath
slab foundation standard;
crawl space or basement available for a fee

ROSEPORT
This is the perfect home with an eye-catching exterior and a charming covered porch. The living room is open to the kitchen, while the cheerful bayed breakfast area adjoins the kitchen via a pass-through snack bar. The roomy bedrooms also have walk-in closets.

PLAN #C19-007D-0109
888 square feet of living area
width: 35'   depth: 38'
2 bedrooms, 1 bath
basement foundation

AUBREY
Step into this compact cottage from the inviting covered front porch and discover a pleasant great room with enough space for entertaining. The spacious kitchen/dining area is just steps away and offers a functional layout for comfortable cooking and dining.

PLAN #C19-121D-0033
944 square feet of living area
width: 32'   depth: 34'
2 bedrooms, 1 bath
basement, crawl space, or slab foundation, please specify when ordering

SOLANGE
The Solange cottage's sloped ceiling in the great room adds a dramatic touch and specious feel to the interior. The organized kitchen has everything close for easy meal prep time.

PLAN #C19-060D-0013
1053 square feet of living area
width: 24'-9"   depth: 46'-9"
3 bedrooms, 2 baths
crawl space or slab foundation, please specify when ordering

BRIARIDGE
The Briaridge cottage enjoys shady porches for relaxing evenings. The living room and dining area are open to an L-shaped kitchen. The bedroom has a full bath, walk-in closet, and rear porch access.

PLAN #C19-007D-0199
496 square feet of living area
width: 39'   depth: 33'
1 bedroom, 1 bath
slab foundation

SPRINGDALE

A stylish cottage retreat, the Springdale cottage has a delightful country porch, perfect for quiet evenings. The living room offers an arched front feature window inviting the sun indoors and includes a fireplace, dining area, and private patio access.

PLAN #C19-007D-0105
1084 square feet of living area
width: 35' depth: 40'-8"
2 bedrooms, 2 baths
basement foundation

BRANSON BLUFF

The perfect country retreat, featuring a vaulted entry and impressive living room with skylights and a plant shelf. The kitchen has generous storage and a pass-through breakfast bar. Double-doors lead to a vaulted bedroom with bath access.

PLAN #C19-007D-0029
576 square feet of living area
width: 24' depth: 30'
1 bedroom, 1 bath
crawl space foundation

COTSWOLD

This cottage's charm is achieved thanks to gables, decorative trim, Old English windows, a balcony, flower boxes, and lanterns. Inside, find a sunken living area with a cozy wood-burning fireplace.

PLAN #C19-007D-0217
1075 square feet of living area
width: 38' depth: 34'
1 bedroom, 1 bath
crawl space foundation

CASCADE BAY

This cottage enjoys a two-story vaulted living area with combined kitchen. Above, a roomy loft overlooks to below. There's also covered front and back porches for unwinding in the shade.

PLAN #C19-152D-0028
860 square feet of living area
width: 20' depth: 46'
1 bedroom, 1 bath
2" x 6" exterior walls
slab foundation

ROLLINS
The Rollins cottage has so many great features including a two-story living room with clerestory windows above, a breakfast bar for three people plus a nearby dinette, a study alcove under the stairs, a laundry room, and a private second floor bedroom.

PLAN #C19-130D-0363
597 square feet of living area
width: 16'   depth: 29'
1 bedroom, 1 bath
slab foundation standard;
basement or crawl space available for a fee

BERRYBRIDGE
The covered front porch will see many days and nights of summer enjoyment. Step into the living room with a warm fireplace and a nearby kitchen with a door to the backyard. The bedrooms are private with lots of closet space.

PLAN #C19-008D-0159
733 square feet of living area
width: 30'   depth: 32'
2 bedrooms, 1 bath
pier foundation

Blueprint PRICING and ORDERING + VISIT houseplansandmore.com + 1-800-373-2646

OAK COVE
The Oak Cove cottage is outfitted with a covered porch, creating a place to relax in nature. The family room is warmed by a fireplace, while the kitchen has a pantry and the bath has washer/dryer space.

PLAN #C19-040D-0029
1028 square feet of living area
width: 30'   depth: 30'-6"
3 bedrooms, 1 bath
crawl space foundation

HERONPOND
Heronpond cottage transports you to the Lowcountry and begs you to invite neighbors for a crawfish boil. The covered front porch is a great outdoor escape. The kitchen has casual dining space.

PLAN #C19-020D-0330
569 square feet of living area
width: 20'   depth: 39'
1 bedroom, 1 bath
2" x 6" exterior walls
crawl space or slab foundation,
please specify when ordering

VACATION HOME MAINTENANCE

If you're lucky enough to own a vacation home, then you probably long for the moment when you can escape your daily routine and head to this special place. Vacation homes provide a mental escape located in a tranquil place away from the errands, carpooling, and all of the headaches associated with running a household every day. Whether you have a cabin on the lake or a beachfront cottage, being only a temporary resident can pose some special problems and maintenance issues for a homeowner. Here are some important things to remember when trying to maintain a home while you are away.

SECURITY

It can be a difficult task keeping your home safe and secure when you're not there. Daily activity and the presence of those who dwell there are an automatic safeguard from theft and vandalism. The minute you leave, your precious home is at risk.

Here are a few easy and inexpensive ways to keep your home from looking vulnerable.

+ Add automatic lights that are on a timer or can be controlled remotely with an app from your smart phone. Having lights surrounding the exterior will make those who are interested in breaking in less comfortable about acting it out. Also, have interior lamps or lights to turn on regularly, which will keep up the appearance of regular activity. Have a kitchen lamp turn on early in the evening and possibly a bedroom lamp remain on later into the night.

+ If you have a friend that lives near your vacation home, have them occasionally drive by and survey the area. If they know your patterns and routines, they will be sure to notice if anything looks out of place almost immediately.

+ Even if the home is not used on a regular basis, it is still important to keep it maintained and clean so it is ready to be enjoyed the minute you arrive. Consider hiring a cleaning service to keep up your home in-between visits and protect the interior from dust and mold. Plus, having routine visitors lets intruders know the home is well-kept and cared for by the owners.

+ Installing a security system is another way to ensure your favorite getaway is safe. Although there will be some costs involved with installation, typically the monthly or quarterly payments for the service are relatively inexpensive.

MAINTENANCE

Proper heating, cooling, and other maintenance measures need to be  considered even when the home is not in use. Not having the interior set on a proper temperature can cause damage to pipes, flooring, and other areas. Here are several maintenance ideas to keep your home welcoming when you arrive for a week of fun and relaxation.

HVAC – In the winter, the ideal temperature for keeping your home safe from frozen pipes is between 50 and 55 degrees. During the summer, be sure the interior does not become overheated. If your home gets too hot or too moist, mold and rust can occur.

Appliances – If you will not be visiting your vacation cabin or cottage for a while, consider unplugging appliances. Many fires have been attributed to everyday appliances with faulty wiring. Unplugging automatically eliminates this hazard.

Pests – Secure windows, patch up holes, and install mesh over attic vents and soffits to keep mice, squirrels, and birds out. Who wants to show up for a relaxing vacation and discover you'll be sharing it with these creatures? It's a lot easier to keep them out than it is to find a way to remove them once they're in.

Protect Outdoor Furniture – Cover outdoor furniture to reduce the possibility of storm damage. Shut down your gas grill to avoid leaks and chain it to a railing to keep it from blowing away during an intense storm. Securing everything outdoors will keep damage to your home's siding and windows at a minimum.

These special maintenance tips and ideas will make your visits to your special vacation getaway enjoyable and stress-free. Taking these simple steps before you leave will keep from unexpected disasters presenting themselves when you return the next time.

VACATION
HOMES

Plan #C19-126D-0992 is found on page 86.

Vacation homes come in a wide variety of styles, but these dwellings are often found in waterfront, coastal, or mountain locations, perfect for getting away from it all and taking a much needed break from reality. Many vacation-style homes are designed for carefree living, typically are smaller in size and feature efficient, open floor plans and plenty of large windows to easily enjoy surrounding views, and are designed for a sloping lot. With a diverse selection of styles and sizes, there is a vacation home waiting for everyone.

PLATEAU PEAK VACATION HOME

Plateau Peak is a rugged modern mountain escape offering a private getaway ideal for views of all kinds. With windows everywhere, this rustic cabin proves that no angle is out of sight. Step in from the covered porch and find a main gathering space with a kitchen on one wall, allowing the cabin to remain entirely open. The bedroom is steps away and has a full bath outside its doors. When life takes over, grab a bag and head here to completely recharge from the daily grind.

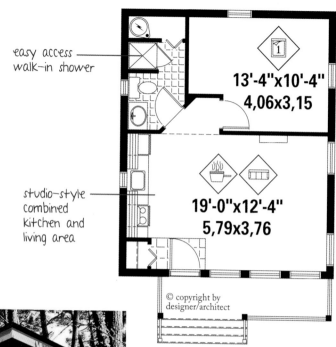

easy access
walk-in shower

studio-style
combined
kitchen and
living area

13'-4"x10'-4"
4,06x3,15

19'-0"x12'-4"
5,79x3,76

© copyright by
designer/architect

PLAN #C19-126D-0992

480 square feet of living area
width: 20'   depth: 24'
1 bedroom, 1 bath
2" x 6" exterior walls
crawl space foundation

PAULINE VACATION HOME

Step onto this charming front porch that is sure to open into a home just as charming. The family room, dining area, and kitchen transition seamlessly into one another for an open and spacious interior design. There is plenty of storage in this home with many closets and pantries. The master bedroom has a generous closet with plenty of floor space. All of the bedrooms access a well-equipped bath featuring a whirlpool tub, a relaxing shower, and a large vanity for optimal storage space.

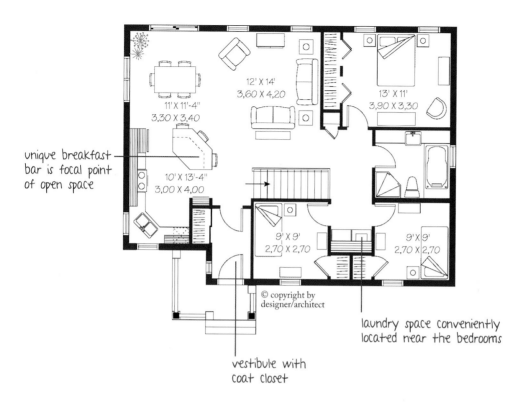

11' X 11'-4"
3,30 X 3,40

12' X 14'
3,60 X 4,20

13' X 11'
3,90 X 3,30

unique breakfast
bar is focal point
of open space

10' 13'-4"
3,00 X 4,00

9' X 9'
2,70 X 2,70

9' X 9'
2,70 X 2,70

© copyright by
designer/architect

laundry space conveniently
located near the bedrooms

vestibule with
coat closet

PLAN #C19-032D-0732

1160 square feet of living area
width: 40'   depth: 30'
3 bedrooms, 1 bath
2" x 6" exterior walls
basement foundation standard;
crawl space, floating slab, or monolithic slab
available for a fee

SHERIDAN PARK VACATION HOME

The Sheridan Park is an energy-efficient vacation home that has a large two-story window wall that commands full attention upon entering the living area and creates the perfect opportunity to spotlight surrounding views, whether lakeside or tucked in the mountains. A compact yet convenient eating bar offers a quick meal solution right off of the open kitchen floor plan. Meanwhile, the second floor sleeping loft enjoys lots of natural sunlight during the daytime and a quiet place at night to catch some shut-eye.

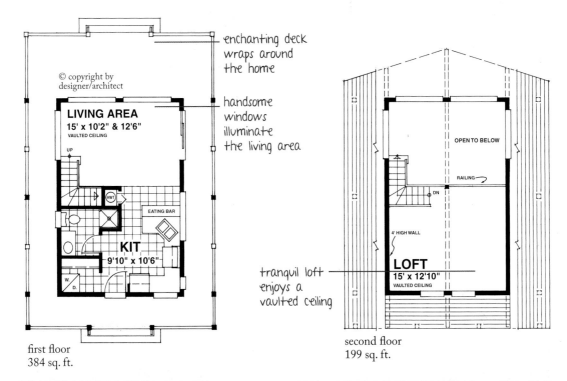

© copyright by
designer/architect

LIVING AREA
15' x 10'2" & 12'6"
VAULTED CEILING

UP

HWT

EATING BAR

KIT
9'10" x 10'6"

W. D.

enchanting deck
wraps around
the home

handsome
windows
illuminate
the living area

first floor
384 sq. ft.

OPEN TO BELOW

RAILING

DN

4' HIGH WALL

LOFT
15' x 12'10"
VAULTED CEILING

tranquil loft
enjoys a
vaulted ceiling

second floor
199 sq. ft.

PLAN #C19-080D-0001

583 square feet of living area
width: 24'   depth: 36'
1 bedroom, 1 bath
2" x 6" exterior walls
crawl space foundation

ISLAND VIEW VACATION HOME

Island View vacation home is the place to spend tranquil weekends by the shore. The breezy covered porch with a wood stove is an outdoor space that can be utilized all year long. Multiple sliding glass doors lead to a living area with a fireplace and an efficient galley kitchen. The bedroom has an entire wall of windows so you can be awakened naturally by the sun, and it also enjoys its own private bath. You have found your very own paradise, so start packing your bags!

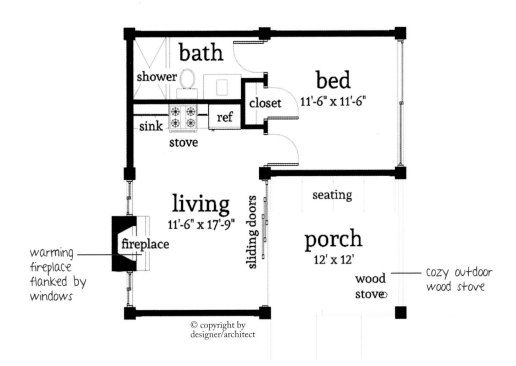

bath

shower

bed
11'-6" x 11'-6"

closet

sink

ref

stove

living
11'-6" x 17'-9"

fireplace

warming fireplace flanked by windows

sliding doors

seating

porch
12' x 12'

wood stove

cozy outdoor wood stove

© copyright by designer/architect

PLAN #C19-152D-0048

456 square feet of living area
width: 25'   depth: 25'
1 bedroom, 1 bath
2" x 6" exterior walls
pilings foundation

WATERVISTA VACATION HOME

Whether you spend a weekend canoeing or having s'mores out by the fire pit, this bungalow-style cabin is the perfect humble abode you've always wanted to escape to. With its welcoming covered front porch for enjoying morning coffee, you'll discover that views can be seen in all directions. The main gathering space merges dining, cooking, and relaxing together, making the home feel inviting and larger than its true size. Two bedrooms also share a central bath for extra convenience. Grab your family and friends and have a fun-filled weekend at Watervista!

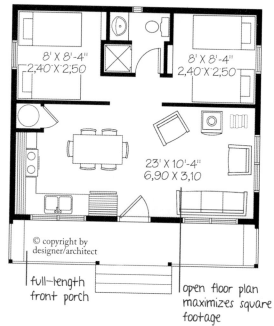

8' X 8'-4"
2,40 X 2,50

8' X 8'-4"
2,40 X 2,50

23' X 10'-4"
6,90 X 3,10

© copyright by
designer/architect

full-length
front porch

open floor plan
maximizes square
footage

PLAN #C19-032D-0709

480 square feet of living area
width: 24'   depth: 20'
2 bedrooms, 1 bath
2" x 6" exterior walls
screw pile foundation standard;
crawl space, floating slab, or monolithic slab
available for a fee

JUNO BAY
VACATION HOME

Juno Bay is a stunning, modern-style, multi-level vacation home offering privacy for the homeowner with the master bedroom located on the top floor and featuring its own walk-in closet, private bath, and sunning deck. The first floor is one large space that is composed of dining, living, and cooking areas. Parties will be relaxing and fun thanks to the ease in which you can move through this space. This floor leads onto a partially covered balcony that is sure to be a focal point. It will be the perfect spot for alfresco dining, sunbathing, or happy hour with guests. An optional lower level can be finished as needed and provides an additional 512 square feet of living area and offers the ability to add another living area, as well as two additional bedrooms and a bath.

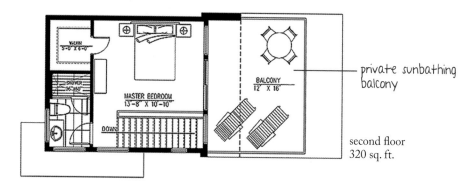

private sunbathing balcony

second floor
320 sq. ft.

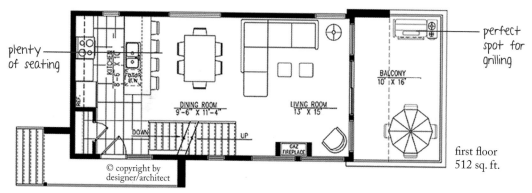

plenty of seating

perfect spot for grilling

first floor
512 sq. ft.

© copyright by
designer/architect

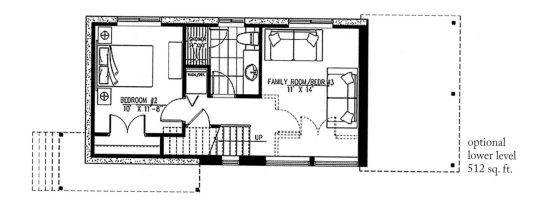

optional
lower level
512 sq. ft.

PLAN #C19-148D-0032

832 square feet of living area
512 bonus square feet
width: 16' depth: 32'
1 bedroom, 1 bath
2" x 6" exterior walls
walk-out basement foundation

DUCK BLIND VACATION HOME

Pack up for the weekend and stay at the Duck Blind vacation spot, where you can hunt, fish, or just enjoy nature to the fullest. This raised cottage offers luxury for its size that includes a small kitchen with dining space, a large bedroom with two closets, and a luxury bath featuring an oversized walk-in shower and a freestanding tub. There is also a wonderful covered porch, perfect for relaxing and dining outdoors without the heat of direct sunlight. Sneak away to the Duck Blind and come back refreshed and ready for another week!

luxurious bathroom

huge covered porch

© copyright by designer/architect

PLAN #C19-152D-0055

477 square feet of living area
width: 33'   depth: 29'
1 bedroom, 1 bath
2" x 6" exterior walls
pilings foundation

BAGNELL LAKE VACATION HOME

Everyone will head on the weekends to the Bagnell Lake vacation home that is sure to be the envy of the cove. Designed perfectly for a sloping lot, the large vaulted living room with fireplace overlooks a huge outdoor deck. The corner kitchen is nearby so outdoor grilling and dining is easy. There's a bedroom on the first floor, and two bedrooms and a bath on the second floor. The basement can be finished to offer more bedroom or gathering space when larger crowds are invited.

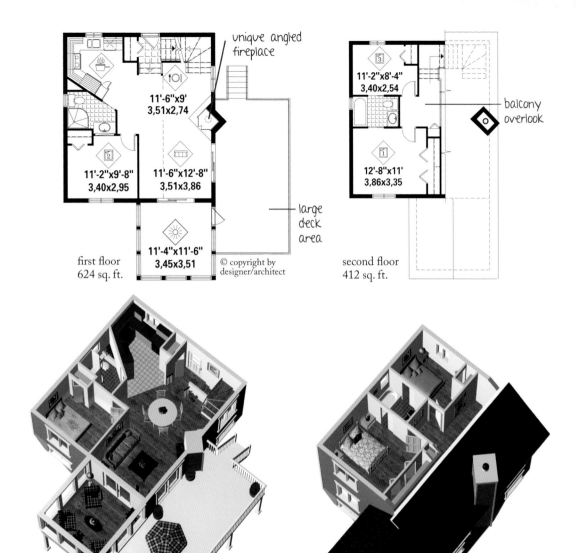

unique angled fireplace

11'-6"x9'
3,51x2,74

11'-2"x9'-8"
3,40x2,95

11'-6"x12'-8"
3,51x3,86

11'-4"x11'-6"
3,45x3,51

first floor
624 sq. ft.

© copyright by
designer/architect

large
deck
area

11'-2"x8'-4"
3,40x2,54

balcony
overlook

12'-8"x11'
3,86x3,35

second floor
412 sq. ft.

PLAN #C19-126D-1029

1036 square feet of living area
width: 24'   depth: 26'
3 bedrooms, 2 baths
2" x 6" exterior walls
basement foundation

TUCSON RETREAT VACATION HOME

Looking for your own private desert oasis? This ultra-modern home offers the most private layout. The first floor has a common living space with small kitchen surrounded in windows for great patio views. The garage is separate but shares the patio for easy access. The second floor is two completely separate spaces, each with its own entrance, full bath, and walk-in closet. Enjoy the tranquility of this modern dwelling and offer the utmost privacy for yourself and your guests. There's even space designated for a pool with an unforgettable waterfall wall.

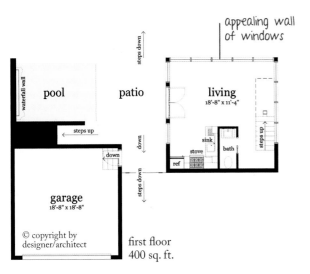

appealing wall of windows

steps down

waterfall wall

pool   patio   living
18'-8" x 11'-4"

steps up

down

steps up

sink

stove

ref   bath

steps down

down

garage
18'-8" x 18'-8"

© copyright by
designer/architect

first floor
400 sq. ft.

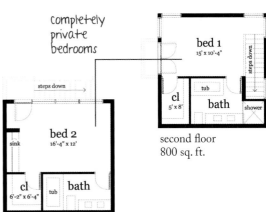

completely private bedrooms

bed 1
15' x 10'-4"

steps down

steps down

cl
5' x 8'   bath   shower

tub

second floor
800 sq. ft.

bed 2
16'-4" x 12'

sink

cl
6'-2" x 6'-4"   tub   bath

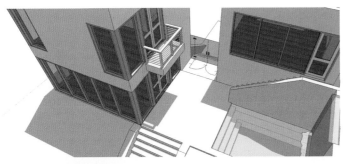

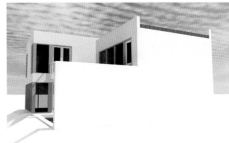

PLAN #C19-152D-0039

1200 square feet of living area
width: 49' depth: 38'
2 bedrooms, 2½ baths
2" x 6" exterior walls
slab foundation

KRESSLEY VACATION HOME

The Kressley vacation home features a prominent gazebo located in the rear for superb outdoor living and elevated views, making this plan ideal for a sloping lakeside lot. Lots of windows create a cheerful and sunny atmosphere throughout this entire vacation home. Plus, the open floor plan is exactly what homeowners love. The kitchen, dining, and living rooms all combine for the most optimal usable floor plan. Plus, the enormous bathroom has a corner oversized tub.

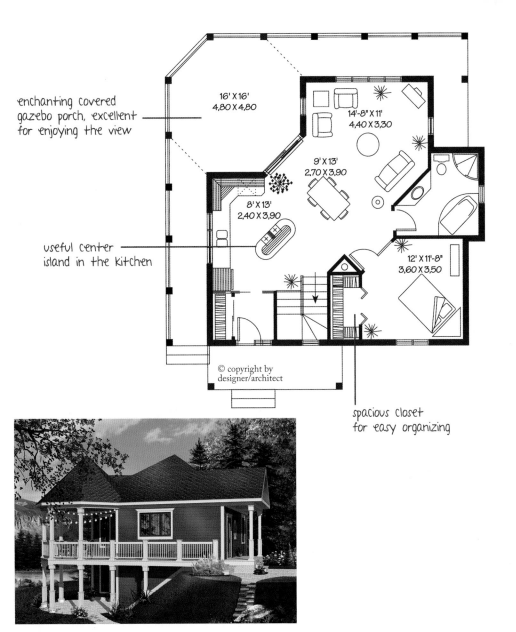

enchanting covered gazebo porch, excellent for enjoying the view

16' X 16'
4,80 X 4,80

14'-8" X 11'
4,40 X 3,30

9' X 13'
2,70 X 3,90

8' X 13'
2,40 X 3,90

useful center island in the kitchen

12' X 11'-8"
3,60 X 3,50

© copyright by designer/architect

spacious closet for easy organizing

PLAN #C19-032D-0050

840 square feet of living area
width: 33'   depth: 31'
1 bedroom, 1 bath
2" x 6" exterior walls
walk-out basement standard;
crawl space, floating slab, or monolithic slab
available for a fee

WOODBRIDGE

The Woodbridge is a great starter or vacation home, with its completely open living and dining areas making it feel larger than its actual size. The convenient U-shaped kitchen has a breakfast bar, and there's a handy laundry area. The living/dining area opens to a spacious deck where enjoying the outdoors is a breeze. Quite possibly the perfect cabin!

PLAN #C19-001D-0086

1154 square feet of living area
width: 28'   depth: 38'
3 bedrooms, 1 1/2 baths
basement, crawl space, or slab foundation, please specify when ordering

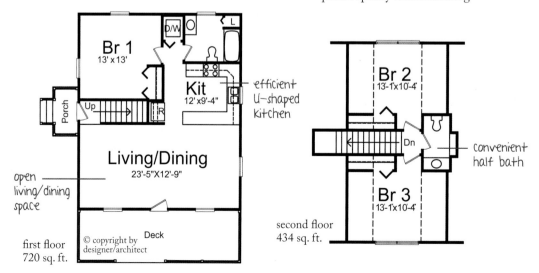

Br 1
13' x 13'

Kit
12' x9'-4"

efficient
U-shaped
kitchen

Living/Dining
23'-5"X12'-9"

open
living/dining
space

Porch

Up

first floor
720 sq. ft.

© copyright by
designer/architect

Deck

Br 2
13'-1x10-4'

convenient
half bath

Br 3
13'-1x10-4'

Dn

second floor
434 sq. ft.

ALFREDO LAGO

PLAN #C19-011D-0291

972 square feet of living area
width: 49'-6"   depth: 31'-6"
1 bedroom, 1 bath
2" x 6" exterior walls
joisted crawl space or post & beam standard;
slab or basement available for a fee

Dreaming of an Italian villa high in the hills of wine country? Look no further than this Tuscan-inspired villa with the romance and character to create the feeling of complete bliss in a faraway place. A pergola-style outdoor living space has multiple sliding glass doors leading to the living room with a freestanding fireplace. A sizable kitchen with eating bar makes Italian recipes a cinch, and the bedroom is spacious with direct bath access. Feel as though you've been whisked away in stunning Tuscan style!

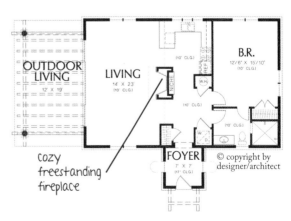

cozy freestanding fireplace

YAKUTAT

Memorable family events are certain to be enjoyed on the partially covered deck of the Yakutat vacation home. The living area is topped with a cathedral ceiling and rafters for a dramatic, open feel. A kitchenette, bedroom, and bath complete the first floor, while a second floor loft is accessible by an incline ladder. Relaxing is sure to be a breeze in this retreat-like A-frame home.

PLAN #C19-008D-0161

618 square feet of living area
width: 20'   depth: 30'
1 bedroom, 1 bath
pier foundation

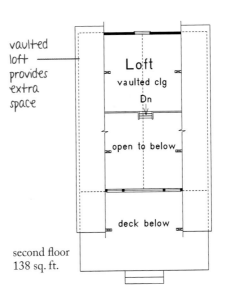

grand
2-story
living room

delightful
partially
covered deck

Br 1
9'-4"x11'-6"

Kit

Living
18'x11'-4"
vaulted clg

Up

Covered Deck

first floor
480 sq. ft.

© copyright by
designer/architect

vaulted
loft
provides
extra
space

Loft
vaulted clg

Dn

open to below

deck below

second floor
138 sq. ft.

SCENIC RETREAT

PLAN #C19-155D-0012

1098 square feet of living area
width: 28'-6"   depth: 56'
2 bedrooms, 2 baths
2" x 6" exterior walls
crawl space or slab foundation,
please specify when ordering

The Scenic Retreat vacation home has multiple decks and an open floor plan creating a vacation home that always feels inviting and ready for fun. The great room has a freestanding fireplace separating it from the kitchen. Plus, there's a walk-in pantry, perfect for staples, appliances, and storage. The second floor sleeping loft overlooks all of the action below and is spacious enough for a few beds, so you're always ready for extra guests on short notice.

functional laundry room

© copyright by designer/architect

breathtaking wall of windows

first floor 883 sq. ft.

second floor 215 sq. ft.

comfy sleeping loft

HICKORY GROVE

The Hickory Grove has a welcoming covered front porch with two stunning columns supporting a charming balcony above. The romantic master suite boasts a bay window, ample closet space, and a nearby full bath with a relaxing shower. On the second floor, the cozy family room has a massive corner fireplace, multiple windows, and an open floor plan flowing freely into the kitchen. This is a great inverted layout if you need a little height to better optimize your surrounding views.

PLAN #C19-032D-0512

1088 square feet of living area
width: 22'   depth: 26'
2 bedrooms, 2 baths
2" x 6" exterior walls
floating slab or basement foundation standard; crawl space or monolithic slab available for a fee

© copyright by designer/architect

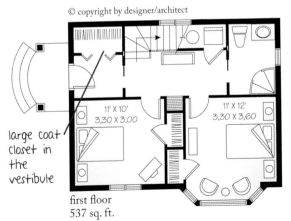

large coat closet in the vestibule

11' X 10'
3,30 X 3,00

11' X 12'
3,30 X 3,60

first floor
537 sq. ft.

warming gas corner fireplace

14' X 15'
4,20 X 4,50

11' X 12'-8"
3,30 X 3,80

second floor
551 sq. ft.

SERENE HILLS

PLAN #C19-126D-0088

1092 square feet of living area
width: 34'   depth: 26'
1 bedroom, 2 baths
2" x 6" exterior walls
basement foundation

Serene Hills is a special modern, rustic retreat that is sure to make a lasting impression. From the moment you arrive, you will be impressed by the unique, angular exterior. Inside, a see-through fireplace on the first floor is shared by both the dining and living spaces. A compact yet functional kitchen offers all the essentials you need. The second floor bedroom is a romantic retreat with a huge fireplace and an open private bath with an oversized whirlpool tub.

© copyright by designer/architect

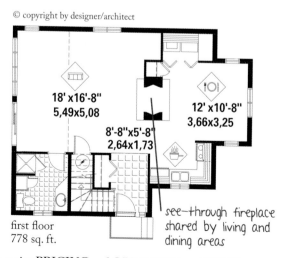

18' x16'-8"
5,49x5,08

8'-8"x5'-8"
2,64x1,73

12' x10'-8"
3,66x3,25

first floor
778 sq. ft.

see-through fireplace
shared by living and
dining areas

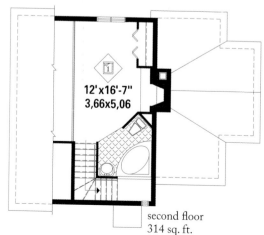

12' x16'-7"
3,66x5,06

second floor
314 sq. ft.

CLAIRE BEACH

Retreat to Claire Beach and find your happy place. The modern, sleek style will make living uncomplicated and less stressful. The vaulted living area is two stories tall with towering windows so you can enjoy views of the beach or lake shore. Two bedrooms, one on each floor, offer maximum privacy.

PLAN #C19-126D-1037

1165 square feet of living area
width: 26'   depth: 28'
2 bedrooms, 2¹/₂ baths
2" x 6" exterior walls
basement foundation

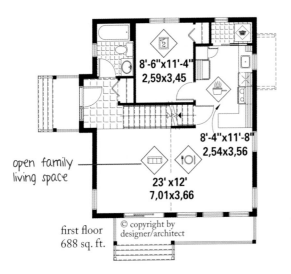

8'-6"x11'-4"
2,59x3,45

open family
living space

8'-4"x11'-8"
2,54x3,56

23' x12'
7,01x3,66

first floor
688 sq. ft.

© copyright by
designer/architect

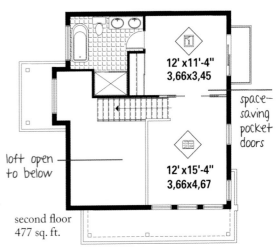

12' x11'-4"
3,66x3,45

space-
saving
pocket
doors

loft open
to below

12' x15'-4"
3,66x4,67

second floor
477 sq. ft.

YUKON

PLAN #C19-008D-0162

865 square feet of living area
width: 26'   depth: 36'
2 bedrooms, 1 bath
pier foundation

The living area of the Yukon provides an enormous amount of space for gathering around the large, roaring fireplace. The kitchen is bright and cheerful with multiple windows and direct deck access. Two bedrooms complete the second floor. Plus, an outdoor ladder on the wraparound deck connects the top deck with the first floor deck in an unforgettable fashion.

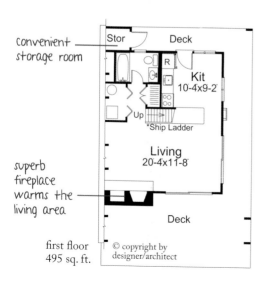

convenient storage room

Stor

Deck

Kit
10-4x9-2

R

Up
*Ship Ladder

Living
20-4x11-8

superb fireplace warms the living area

Deck

first floor
495 sq. ft.

© copyright by designer/architect

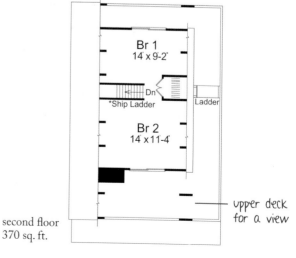

Br 1
14' x 9-2'

Dn
*Ship Ladder

Ladder

Br 2
14' x 11-4'

upper deck for a view

second floor
370 sq. ft.

BIG SKY PEAK

The Big Sky Peak is a modern masterpiece perfect for great views, whether mountain or coastal. With its huge deck and wall of windows, no view is left unseen. The first floor includes an island kitchen as well as the master bedroom and a full bath. An optional lower level doubles the square footage and includes three additional bedrooms, a large bath, and washer/dryer closet.

PLAN #C19-148D-0047

720 square feet of living area
width: 30'   depth: 24'
1 bedroom, 1 bath
2" x 6" exterior walls
basement foundation

useful carport

double bowl vanity

© copyright by designer/architect

optional lower level 720 sq. ft.

first floor 720 sq. ft.

JUNIPER COVE

PLAN #C19-126D-1022

1156 square feet of living area
width: 24'   depth: 28'
2 bedrooms, 1 bath
2" x 6" exterior walls
basement foundation

Juniper Cove offers the perfect setup for lakeside living since it's designed ideally for a sloping lot. With a layout perfect for rear views, the bedrooms all enjoy balconies or large windows for catching sunsets over the water. Window walls make guests and family feel one with nature even if they're indoors by the fire.

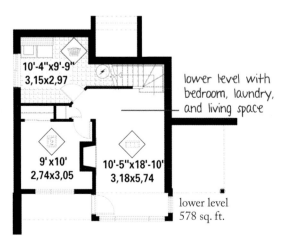

10'-4"x9'-9"
3,15x2,97

lower level with bedroom, laundry, and living space

9' x 10'
2,74x3,05

10'-5"x18'-10"
3,18x5,74

lower level
578 sq. ft.

large walk-in storage closet

© copyright by designer/architect

11'-6"x10'
3,51x3,05

11' x 8'
3,35x2,44

first floor
578 sq. ft.

SHADYBRIDGE LAKE This
low-maintenance cottage offers vacation living with 2" x 6" exterior walls. The living/dining area merges with the kitchen. Easy access bath to the bedroom. This plan also has an uninsulated/unheated version for seasonal use only.

PLAN #C19-032D-0708
400 square feet of living area
width: 20'   depth: 20'
1 bedroom, 1 bath
screw pile foundation standard;
crawl space, monolithic slab, or floating slab available for a fee

SCENIC POINT Modern cabin-style
living has never been easier than Scenic Point. The front screen porch creates ideal outdoor living, while two bedrooms share a full bath with efficient and convenient washer/dryer space.

PLAN #C19-126D-1018
900 square feet of living area
width: 30'   depth: 42'
2 bedrooms, 1 bath
2" x 6" exterior walls
basement foundation

JACINTO The large covered porch offers a
tranquil spot to take in the surrounding views. Inside, an expansive living/dining area is open to the kitchen, creating an ideal entertaining spot with its center island eating bar.

PLAN #C19-057D-0034
1020 square feet of living area
width: 34'-8"   depth: 40'
2 bedrooms, 1 bath
2" x 6" exterior walls
basement foundation

WINDFALL RIDGE This cozy,
quaint cabin has 2" x 6" exterior walls and Craftsman details, making it irresistible. One gathering area with a centered fireplace blends with the kitchen for relaxed cabin living.

PLAN #C19-032D-0710
540 square feet of living area
width: 18'   depth: 30'
2 bedrooms, 1 bath
screw pile foundation standard;
crawl space, monolithic slab, or floating slab available for a fee

HIGHLANDER
The perfect cabin for comfort and utility. Abundant windows in the gathering area provide sunlight throughout. The U-shaped kitchen has a breakfast bar opening to the living area. The large covered deck offers plenty of outdoor living space.

PLAN #C19-001D-0085
720 square feet of living area
width: 28'   depth: 38'
2 bedrooms, 1 bath
crawl space foundation standard;
slab available for a fee

BASS HARBOR
This friendly Craftsman bungalow has a rear covered porch off the well-planned kitchen, offering a great location for a grill. The open dining area flows into the family room with fireplace. A walk-in closet and private bath are found in the master bedroom.

PLAN #C19-026D-1833
1195 square feet of living area
width: 40'   depth: 48'-8"
3 bedrooms, 2 baths
basement foundation standard;
crawl space, slab, or walk-out basement available for a fee

STILLBROOK
What a great getaway with all the comforts of home! A wraparound covered deck and transomed glass doors fill the interior with light. The kitchen/dining/living area has sloped ceilings.

PLAN #C19-008D-0153
792 square feet of living area
width: 24'   depth: 42'
2 bedrooms, 1 bath
crawl space or slab foundation,
please specify when ordering

MONTPELIER
An efficient vestibule separates the front door from the interior. The living area enjoys a vaulted ceiling and the kitchen has a built-in breakfast bar for quick meals on the go.

PLAN #C19-032D-0084
1079 square feet of living area
width: 34'   depth: 34'
2 bedrooms, 1 bath
2" x 6" exterior walls
basement foundation standard; crawl space, monolithic slab, or floating slab available for a fee

RADKO
Small and efficient, this modern studio provides a living/sleeping space with a kitchen wall creating great function. A full bath completes the space and makes it completely self-sufficient as an in-law suite or guest quarters.

PLAN #C19-011D-0305
600 square feet of living area
width: 20' depth: 30'
1 bedroom, 1 bath
2" x 6" exterior walls
joisted crawl space foundation standard;
slab or basement available for a fee

TARANTINO PALM
With two covered porches, homeowners will enjoy comfortable outdoor living. The living room is open to a kitchen/dining area large enough for a family-sized table. Two bedrooms and a full bath complete this stylish home.

PLAN #C19-069D-0107
856 square feet of living area
width: 30' depth: 38'
2 bedrooms, 1 bath
crawl space or slab foundation,
please specify when ordering

MOONLIGHT BAY
A great modern cabin with a floor plan filled with natural light and interesting angles. The kitchen has a dining space and a gathering space with corner fireplace off the other side.

PLAN #C19-126D-0988
850 square feet of living area
width: 34' depth: 30'
2 bedrooms, 1 bath
2" x 6" exterior walls
slab foundation

PROCTOR
Striking and sleek, the interior is light and open with a two-story living room, while the exterior walls are 2" x 6" for efficiency. The kitchen has a built-in table and the second floor has two bedrooms.

PLAN #C19-032D-0863
1200 square feet of living area
width: 27'-7" depth: 38'
2 bedrooms, 2 baths
crawl space foundation standard;
monolithic slab or floating slab available for a fee

PORT DELTA
Sliding glass doors provide easy deck access, added sunlight, and great views in this open, vaulted vacation cottage. Two comfortable bedrooms and a bath will make this your favorite spot to be all summer long.

PLAN #C19-126D-1019
924 square feet of living area
width: 24' depth: 40'
2 bedrooms, 1 bath
2" x 6" exterior walls
basement foundation

ALLISON POINT
A wraparound deck and covered porch surround this fun, rustic cabin with tons of space for sunning, grilling and lounging. The vaulted family room soars for an airy feel and the lower level can be finished as needed.

PLAN #C19-141D-0003
765 square feet of living area
792 bonus square feet
width: 32' depth: 48'
1 bedroom, 1 bath
slab foundation

BEAVERHILL
Lots of glass and a low roofline create a retreat you'll be begging to return to. The living room has a fireplace that heats a nearby stone wall for extra warmth. The kitchen has dining space.

PLAN #C19-008D-0133
624 square feet of living area
width: 26' depth: 24'
2 bedrooms, 1 bath
pier foundation

SHADY SLOPE
The perfect option for a sloping lot, whether mountain or lakeside, this home offers a comfortable gathering space, a sunny dining area, and a kitchen with a laundry room.

PLAN #C19-126D-1005
1133 square feet of living area
width: 42' depth: 32'
2 bedrooms, 1 bath
2" x 6" exterior walls
basement foundation

"RIGHT-SIZING" YOUR HOME & LIFE

When you call out to another family member, does your home seem to echo? Are there more spaces that aren't used in your home than are being used? Like many homeowners who once thought "bigger is better," you may be changing your tune. Many of us are changing our ways and learning that downsizing is the way to go. And, thanks to the recession in the not-so-distant past, we have learned that it is possible to have simplicity in our lives, spend less money, and still enjoy a very full life.

Once considered standard practice for empty nesters and retirees only, downsizing is now reaching all ages and incomes and it is for a variety of reasons. Many have chosen to downsize their home because they want a simpler lifestyle with less maintenance. People who love to travel or who are involved with many hobbies outside their home want less clutter and maintenance in their everyday life. Downsizing has also come to the forefront of society because of those who have faced financial difficulties in the past several years. Many homeowners have had no choice but to downsize and rid themselves of expensive mortgages in order to make ends meet. Whatever the situation, there are several advantages to downsizing that may convince you that it is the right choice for you and your family.

ADVANTAGES OF DOWNSIZING

Increased Cash Flow
Whether you shrink your mortgage or you use the proceeds of selling your current home to pay entirely for a new smaller home, you will end up with more money in your pocket for saving, investing, or spending in another way. Cutting your housing costs is an instant way to increase your savings. So, whether you retire in five years or you're just starting out, think about the added security a smaller home will bring to your financial future.

More Time
Less rooms and smaller ones will cut the time it takes to keep your home maintained more than you might think. Use all this free time for something you really enjoy.

Lower Utility Bills

Yes, this goes along with increased cash flow, but typically smaller homes don't have as much wasted space, so you will be living more efficiently. Using less energy while keeping your home comfortable means lower utility bills.

Reduced Consumption of Everything

From electric and gas to furniture and home accessories, if there is no place to put it, you will think twice before buying it. That means you will automatically spend less on food, clothing, and consumer goods, probably without really noticing.

Less Stress

A smaller home means less responsibility with chores, hefty maintenance bills, and other monthly obligations as a homeowner. Those who successfully downsize appear happier when they are no longer overwhelmed by the high demand and expense of a larger home.

YOU'VE MADE YOUR DECISION, NOW WHAT?

Before you put up a For Sale sign on your current home's front lawn, it is wise to understand how you spend your money, so even when you downsize you still don't find yourself financially strapped. Perhaps you and your family spend way too much money going out to dinner. Well, a smaller home will help, but if freeing up some money for your savings or other reasons is your goal, you may have to examine your lifestyle and see if any changes in how you live are in order. This may be the perfect time to decide what you want to spend your money on and then cut out the things that aren't really important to you.

Remember, downsizing and moving isn't easy. It represents a significant change that no doubt will be physically and emotionally draining during the process, but when "right-sizing" into a smaller home, it will be well worth it in the end. Downsizing is meant to simplify your life, not complicate it. So look forward to a clean, clutter-free home that requires less maintenance and less money to maintain making your family's life happier and easier overall.

SMALL
HOMES

Plan #C19-032D-0904 is found on page 132.

Offering everything a homeowner wants in a smaller footprint with less maintenance, small homes are a very popular trend right now. From new modern designs, to timeless traditional styles, homeowners have discovered that less is more and are choosing this as a way of life. If a small home offers the efficiency and function every homeowner needs, then why do you need more? These small homes look great built anywhere, city or country, and they have all the comfort and amenities you've come to expect from our carefully curated collection of home designs.

FARGO FALLS
SMALL HOME

This rustic beauty provides plenty of space in a small amount of square footage. Step into the living/dining space and notice the large amount of windows on one wall adding a tremendous amount of sunlight. A small yet efficient kitchen offers all of the essentials for cooking daily meals. One bedroom is found on the first floor near a full bath, and two other bedrooms and a full bath reside on the second floor for extra privacy. Two additional spaces for storage make this small home easy to downsize to.

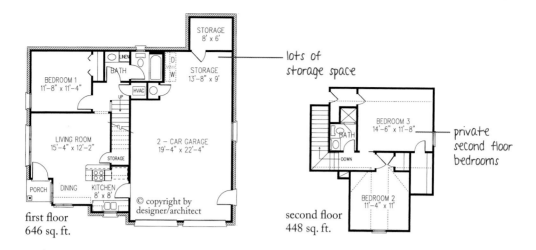

STORAGE
8' x 6'

lots of
storage space

BEDROOM 1
11'-8" x 11'-4"

LINEN

BATH

D
W

STORAGE
13'-8" x 9'

HVAC

UP

BEDROOM 3
14'-6" x 11'-8"

private
second floor
bedrooms

LIVING ROOM
15'-4" x 12'-2"

2 – CAR GARAGE
19'-4" x 22'-4"

BATH

STORAGE

DOWN

PORCH

DINING

KITCHEN
8' x 8'

© copyright by
designer/architect

BEDROOM 2
11'-4" x 11'

first floor
646 sq. ft.

second floor
448 sq. ft.

PLAN #C19-137D-0271

1094 square feet of living area
width: 41'   depth: 40'
3 bedrooms, 2 baths
slab foundation

AMERAULT SMALL HOME

The Amerault ranch home has a super-efficient floor plan that seems to include everything you need for functional living. Double closets in the front entry offer great added storage, which you will also find in the bedrooms. The living and dining areas merge to form the core of the gathering space in the floor plan. A small kitchen has direct backyard access, great when grilling, while the two bedrooms are steps from the full bath with a walk-in shower and a separate tub.

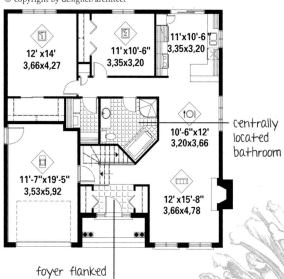

© copyright by designer/architect

◇ 1
12' x14'
3,66x4,27

◇ 2
11' x10'-6"
3,35x3,20

11' x10'-6"
3,35x3,20

◇ ΙΟΙ
10'-6"x12'
3,20x3,66

centrally
located
bathroom

◇ 🚗
11'-7"x19'-5"
3,53x5,92

◇ 🛋
12' x15'-8"
3,66x4,78

foyer flanked
by handy closets

PLAN #C19-126D-0351

1200 square feet of living area
width: 38' depth: 40'
2 bedrooms, 1 bath
2" x 6" exterior walls
basement foundation

CADY LANE
SMALL HOME

Don't be fooled by its tiny looking exterior; this small home has so much style and function you won't miss the square footage. Enter from the covered porch and find an open kitchen with a built-in eating bar. The living area is steps away and opens onto a spacious deck, perfect for summertime entertaining or dining alfresco. The bath features an oversized walk-in shower and a super handy washer and dryer space. A huge walk-in closet completes the bedroom and adds noteworthy storage space. Small home living never seemed so appealing!

expansive deck area

OPEN DECK

© copyright by designer/architect

BEDROOM
10'-6" X 12'

TRANSOM WINDOW

T.V. & DESK AREA

STORAGE

BARN DOOR

LIVING AREA
10'-3" X 12'

LINEN CAB.

WASHER DRYER STACK

BATH

EATING BAR

ROLL-IN SHOWER

KITCHEN
13'-6" X 8'-4"

R.

PORCH

stylish barn door for privacy

PLAN #C19-060D-0606

592 square feet of living area
width: 28'   depth: 21'-2"
1 bedroom, 1 bath
slab foundation

DYSON DOWNS
SMALL HOME

A mix of European cottage and East Coast row home creates the unique Dyson Downs small home, perfectly suited for a small or narrow lot size. This small shingled two-story home would be ideal in an urban or country setting. Almost the entire first floor is the living room and the kitchen is tucked near the stairs. On the second floor, discover a lovely bedroom with a built-in desk and a full bath with a walk-in shower. The 11' ceiling creates the sense of a large space in the bedroom, too. All you need for comfort and ease with very low maintenance!

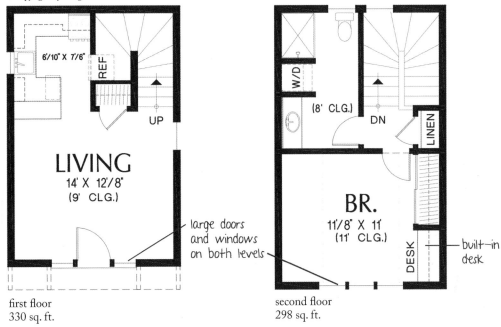

6/10" X 7/6"

REF

UP

LIVING
14' X 12/8"
(9' CLG.)

large doors
and windows
on both levels

first floor
330 sq. ft.

W/D

(8' CLG.)

DN

LINEN

BR.
11/8" X 11'
(11' CLG.)

DESK

built-in
desk

second floor
298 sq. ft.

PLAN #C19-011D-0616

628 square feet of living area
width: 15'   depth: 24'
1 bedroom, 1 bath
2" x 6" exterior walls
joisted crawl space or post & beam foundation
standard; slab or basement available for a fee

EMMIT CREEK
SMALL HOME

Emmit Creek is an ideal layout for a vacation home, or a home for a small family. Its welcoming open interior spaces will feel larger than their true size and create a natural feeling of spaciousness. The kitchen island will offer that much needed prep and extra dining space, maximizing function. Two bedrooms share the full bath tucked between them. This simple yet fluid open-concept floor plan reminds all of us that less is certainly more.

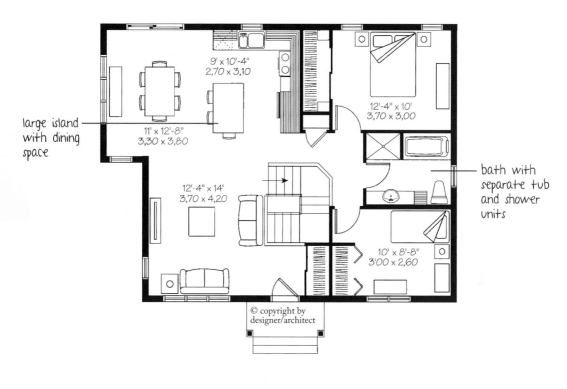

large island
with dining
space

9' x 10'-4"
2,70 x 3,10

11' x 12'-8"
3,30 x 3,80

12'-4" x 10'
3,70 x 3,00

12'-4" x 14'
3,70 x 4,20

bath with
separate tub
and shower
units

10' x 8'-8"
3'00 x 2,60

© copyright by
designer/architect

PLAN #C19-032D-0904

975 square feet of living area
width: 37'   depth: 28'
2 bedrooms, 1 bath
2" x 6" exterior walls
basement foundation standard;
crawl space, floating slab, or monolithic slab
available for a fee

KILLARNEY BAY SMALL HOME

If you're looking for endless country-style charm, then Killarney Bay is just the home for you. A sizable vaulted living area welcomes you inside and flows into the rear kitchen with a spacious area for dining. The luxurious bath includes both a walk-in shower and a garden tub, making this gem of a home a rare find for comfort and unexpected elegance. Two generously sized bedrooms provide plenty of personal space for all of your belongings. There are no sacrifices when living in this small treasure.

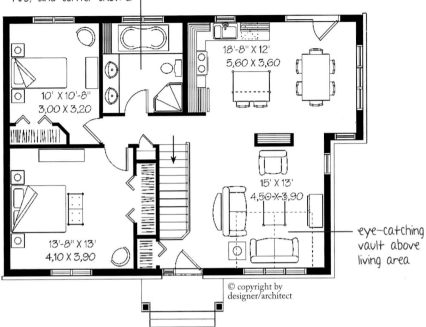

bath with double vanity, tub, and corner shower

10' X 10'-8"
3,00 X 3,20

18'-8" X 12'
5,60 X 3,60

13'-8" X 13'
4,10 X 3,90

15' X 13'
4,50 X 3,90

eye-catching vault above living area

© copyright by designer/architect

PLAN #C19-032D-0945

1068 square feet of living area
width: 40'   depth: 28'
2 bedrooms, 1 bath
2" x 6" exterior walls
basement foundation standard;
crawl space, floating slab, or monolithic slab
available for a fee

MIRANDA MILL SMALL HOME

Miranda Mill is a compact ranch home that provides a open floor plan that merges dining, living, and cooking into one main gathering space. Two bedrooms share a centrally located full bath with ease, and both have a decent amount of closet space. A coat closet is also found by the front entry. Sliding glass doors off the dining area add light and outdoor access. Straightforward and functional, this small home promises to make life easy and comfortable.

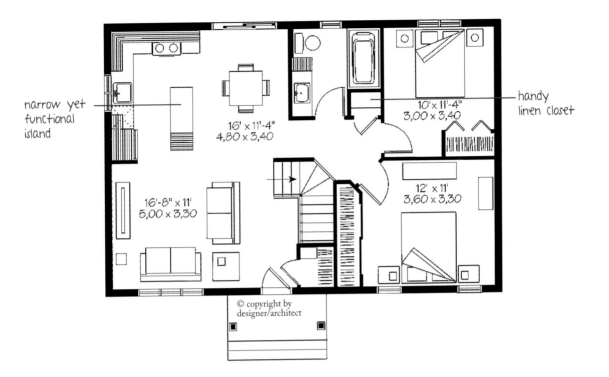

narrow yet functional island

16' x 11'-4"
4,80 x 3,40

handy linen closet

10' x 11'-4"
3,00 x 3,40

16'-8" x 11'
5,00 x 3,30

12' x 11'
3,60 x 3,30

© copyright by designer/architect

PLAN #C19-032D-0984

864 square feet of living area
width: 36'   depth: 24'
2 bedrooms, 1 bath
2" x 6" exterior walls
basement foundation standard;
crawl space, floating slab, or monolithic slab
available for a fee

WENTWORTH BAY SMALL HOME

The Wentworth Bay small home is filled with all of the amenities, inside and out. An attractive wraparound porch accents the exterior of this home. A vestibule keeps unwanted elements outside and also features a large coat closet. There's open family living on the first floor with the living room and kitchen combination. The first floor also comes complete with a full bath. Three bedrooms on the second floor create the perfect quiet place to relax and unwind. This charming and cozy two-story is sure to please any homeowner and offers the best in curb appeal.

11'-8" X 9'
3,50 X 2,70

15'-4" X 14'
4,60 X 4,20

© copyright by
designer/architect

first floor
509 sq. ft.

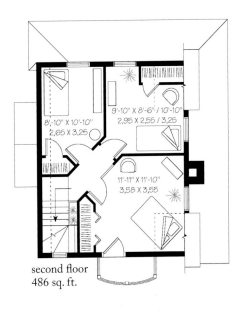

8'-10" X 10'-10"
2,65 X 3,25

9'-10" X 8'-6" / 10'-10"
2,95 X 2,55 / 3,25

11'-11" X 11'-10"
3,58 X 3,55

second floor
486 sq. ft.

PLAN #C19-032D-0897

995 square feet of living area
width: 22'   depth: 24'-4"
3 bedrooms, 1 bath
2" x 6" exterior walls
basement foundation standard;
crawl space, floating slab, or monolithic slab
available for a fee

EUREKA
SMALL HOME

The Eureka berm home is a fresh, modern design that enjoys sleek window lines and a stucco exterior, making it truly efficient and low-maintenance. The compact U-shaped kitchen offers a tremendous amount of counterspace within reach for all sort of kitchen tasks at hand. A tall sloped ceiling in the two-story living room gives this home an open and spacious feel that all those who enter will definitely appreciate. A designated laundry room with pocket doors to a full bath is a highly functional prized feature.

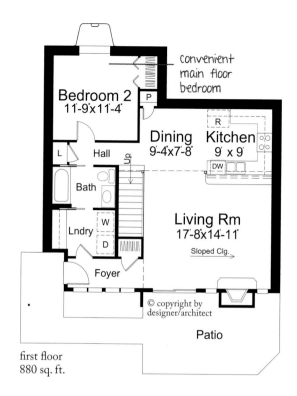

Bedroom 2
11'-9"x11'-4"

convenient main floor bedroom

Dining
9'-4"x7'-8"

Kitchen
9' x 9'

Hall

Bath

Lndry

Up

W

D

Living Rm
17'-8"x14'-11"

Sloped Clg.

Foyer

Patio

first floor
880 sq. ft.

Private bedroom with half bath

Bath

Bedroom 1
11'-10"x14'-2"

Open

Dn

L

second floor
225 sq. ft.

PLAN #C19-122D-0001

1105 square feet of living area
width: 33'   depth: 35'
2 bedrooms, 1½ baths
slab foundation

BRIARWOOD SMALL HOME

The Briarwood is famous for its open and spacious living and dining areas for family gatherings, plus a well-organized kitchen with an abundance of cabinetry and a built-in pantry for ease with storage and when entertaining. There is also a spacious deck, perfect for a grill or outdoor dining. The roomy master bath features a double-bowl vanity. A rear entry drive under garage provides space for two vehicles.

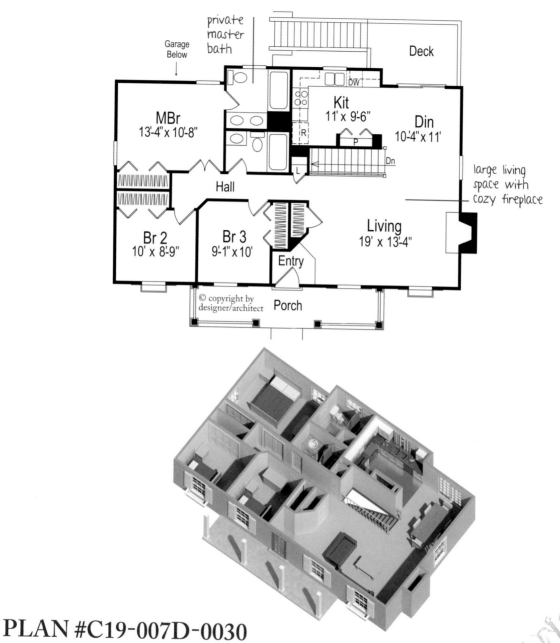

private
master
bath

Garage
Below

Deck

MBr
13'-4" x 10'-8"

Kit
11' x 9'-6"

b/w

Din
10'-4" x 11'

R

P

Dn

L

large living
space with
cozy fireplace

Hall

Br 2
10' x 8'-9"

Br 3
9'-1" x 10'

Living
19' x 13'-4"

Entry

© copyright by
designer/architect

Porch

PLAN #C19-007D-0030

1140 square feet of living area
width: 46'   depth: 32'
3 bedrooms, 2 baths
basement foundation

PARSON FIELD

Looking for your very own Craftsman cottage? Then Parson Field is it! Craftsman details and a covered front porch provide the utmost style and charm. The open living/ dining area enjoys a cozy fireplace and a nearby U-shaped kitchen with a laundry closet near the garage. Upstairs, there are two vaulted bedrooms, a built-in desk, and a well-designed shared bath.

PLAN #C19-011D-0612

803 square feet of living area
width: 29'   depth: 29'
2 bedrooms, $1^{1}/_{2}$ baths
2" x 6" exterior walls
joisted crawl space foundation standard; basement available for a fee

VAULTED
BR. 2
8'2" X 10'

DN.
(8' CLG.)
DESK
B.

VAULTED
BR. 1
9' X 10'4"

second floor
371 sq. ft.

GARAGE
10'6" X 19'

LIVING/
DINING
13'6" X 15'8"+/-
(9' CLG.)

UP

W.
D.

(8' CLG.)

BENCH

REF

8/6X7/4
(9' CLG.)

first floor
432 sq. ft.

© copyright by
designer/architect

OAKHILL

PLAN #C19-045D-0018

858 square feet of living area
width: 20' depth: 21'
2 bedrooms, 1 bath
crawl space foundation

This quaint two-story is perfect for a small- or narrow-size lot. The large covered porch adds curb appeal and opens to a friendly living room with a coat closet. Space for a stackable washer/dryer unit is conveniently located in the dining area/kitchen. Both bedrooms have walk-in closets, too.

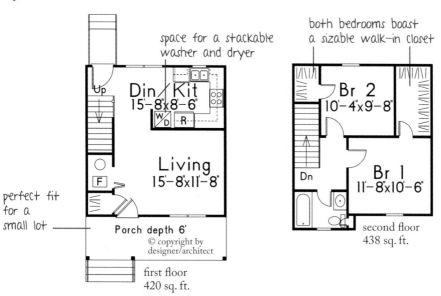

space for a stackable washer and dryer

both bedrooms boast a sizable walk-in closet

Up

Din/Kit
15'-8"x8'-6"

W/D R

Living
15'-8"x11'-8"

F

perfect fit for a small lot

Porch depth 6'
© copyright by designer/architect

first floor
420 sq. ft.

Br 2
10'-4"x9'-8"

Dn

Br 1
11'-8"x10'-6"

second floor
438 sq. ft.

DUNCAN FARM

Duncan Farm has a naturally welcoming feel with its covered front porch. A U-shaped kitchen and adjoining dining room seamlessly transition into the great room making the space feel larger. Double doors open to a rear patio offering space to dine or relax. The master bedroom has a walk-in closet with a private bath and easy entry to the laundry room. Two spare bedrooms have oversized closets for added storage.

PLAN #C19-077D-0208

1200 square feet of living area
width: 50' depth: 43'
3 bedrooms, 2 baths
crawl space or slab foundation,
please specify when ordering

PINECONE

PLAN #C19-008D-0148

784 square feet of living area
width: 28'   depth: 28'
3 bedrooms, 1 bath
pier foundation

Take advantage of panoramic views from several different angles with this A-frame's huge wraparound deck. Upon entering the spacious living area, a cozy freestanding fireplace, a sloped ceiling, and several corner windows catch the eye. Also, the charming kitchen features a peninsula counter. Three bedrooms have direct access to the living room. This is a fun, retro design with all of the appeal of mid-century modern style that's becoming so popular again.

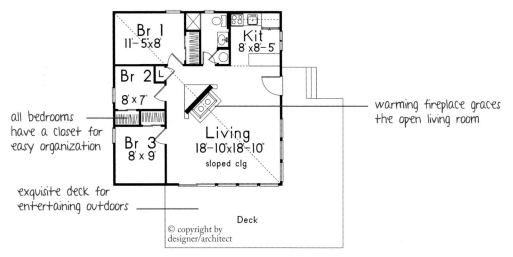

all bedrooms have a closet for easy organization

warming fireplace graces the open living room

exquisite deck for entertaining outdoors

© copyright by designer/architect

Br 1
11'-5"x8'

Kit
8'x8'-5"

Br 2
8'x7'

Br 3
8'x9'

Living
18'-10"x18'-10"
sloped clg

Deck

ROCKPORT

Mid-century modern design in a special smaller size! Step inside the stunning Rockport home and discover a vaulted living room with fireplace and an all-encompassing plant ledge. The vaulted U-shaped kitchen opens to the living area and has a walk-in pantry for keeping the interior clutter-free. The sizable bedroom is near the full bath and laundry closet for ease with chores.

PLAN #C19-011D-0306

899 square feet of living area
width: 34'   depth: 30'
1 bedroom, 1 bath
2" x 6" exterior walls
joisted crawl space or post & beam foundation standard; slab or basement available for a fee

large walk-in pantry

VAULTED
KIT
13/2' X 9/4'

RANGE

REF

PAN

11/2' X 8/4' +/-

LIN.

SPA

MECH.
5/2' X 7/0

(9' CLG.)

BR.
12/0 X 12/4'
(9' CLG.)

PLANT LEDGE

VAULTED
LIVING
16/0 X 12/4'

W/D

© copyright by designer/architect

plant ledge adds character

LAURELWOOD PLACE

PLAN #C19-077D-0106

1200 square feet of living area
width: 30'   depth: 32'
3 bedrooms, 2 baths
SIP exterior walls
crawl space or slab foundation,
please specify when ordering

Laurelwood Place is a great home design with very efficient use of space. This home features covered front and rear porches for enjoying those evening sunsets with family, a screened porch for comfortable dining and entertaining outdoors, a large great room, three bedrooms with walk-in closets, and even a space for the home office that you've always wanted.

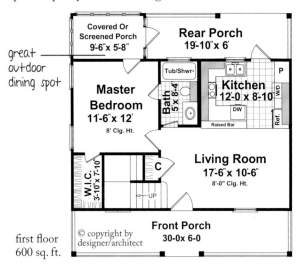

great outdoor dining spot

Covered Or Screened Porch
9'-6" x 5'-8"

Rear Porch
19'-10" x 6'

Master Bedroom
11'-6" x 12'
8' Clg. Ht.

Bath
5' x 8'-4"
Tub/Shwr

Kitchen
12'-0 x 8'-10"
Raised Bar
DW
W/D
P
Ref.

W.I.C.
3'-10" x 7'-10"

C

UP

Living Room
17'-6" x 10'-6"
8'-0" Clg. Ht.

Front Porch
30-0x 6-0

© copyright by designer/architect

first floor
600 sq. ft.

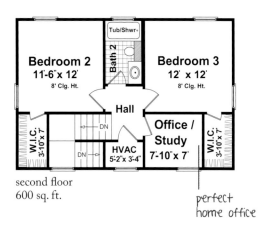

Bedroom 2
11'-6" x 12'
8' Clg. Ht.

Bath 2
Tub/Shwr

Bedroom 3
12' x 12'
8' Clg. Ht.

Hall

W.I.C.
3'-10" x 7'

DN

DN

HVAC
5'-2" x 3'-4"

Office / Study
7'-10" x 7'

W.I.C.
3'-10" x 7'

second floor
600 sq. ft.

perfect home office

TRAILBRIDGE

PLAN #C19-007D-0108

983 square feet of living area
width: 25' depth: 60'
3 bedrooms, 2 baths
crawl space foundation standard;
slab available for a fee

This is an ideal home design for a narrow lot! The Trailbridge small home has a welcoming covered front porch leading you into the adorable living area and relaxing dining area that opens to the well designed kitchen with a convenient breakfast bar. A small side patio with a privacy fence creates an awesome exterior feature and is accessed from the living room. A comfortable master bedroom includes a walk-in closet and a private bath. There's even a handy washer and dryer closet right near all three bedrooms for convenience.

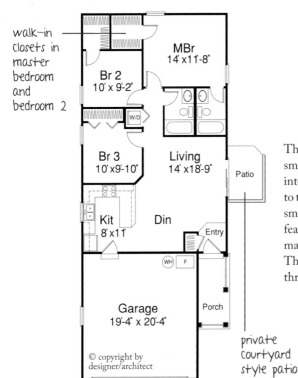

walk-in closets in master bedroom and bedroom 2

MBr
14' x 11'-8"

Br 2
10' x 9'-2"

W/D

Br 3
10' x 9'-10"

Living
14' x 18'-9"

Patio

Kit
8' x 11'

Din

Entry

WH   F

Garage
19'-4" x 20'-4"

Porch

© copyright by designer/architect

private courtyard style patio

TRENTMORE

PLAN #C19-130D-0360

664 square feet of living area
width: 27'   depth: 17'
1 bedroom, 1½ baths
slab foundation standard;
basement or crawl space available for a fee

Charm overload with this two-story tiny home. Perfect as a vacation cottage or getaway place, the Trentmore enjoys a vaulted living room, which makes this home appear larger on the inside than its true size. A kitchen with an island and a nearby dinette are centered with a laundry room and half bath behind it. The vaulted second floor bedroom has its own private bath.

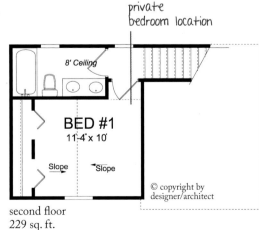

LOTUS

The Lotus small home is a wonderfully modern one-story home featuring today's open-concept floor plan everyone loves. The kitchen, living, and dining areas merge to form the core of this home. A large kitchen island ties the spaces together and creates added function and space when meal prepping. The bathroom includes washer and dryer space as well as a walk-in shower and a garden tub.

PLAN #C19-032D-0905

1146 square feet of living area
width: 40'   depth: 30'
2 bedrooms, 1 bath
2" x 6" exterior walls
basement foundation standard;
crawl space, floating slab, or monolithic slab available for a fee

huge
kitchen island

9'-4" x 11'
2,80 x 3,30

10' x 11'
3,00 x 3,30

10' x 14'
3,00 x 4,20

13' x 13'
3,90 x 3,90

12' x 14'-4"
3,60 x 4,30

© copyright by
designer/architect

GLENCLOVER

PLAN #C19-032D-0911

1186 square feet of living area
width: 50'   depth: 36'
2 bedrooms, 1 bath
2" x 6" exterior walls
basement foundation standard;
crawl space, floating slab, or monolithic slab
available for a fee

The Glenclover small home has nonstop curb appeal with its covered front porch and symmetrical gables. A vaulted living area shares a three-sided fireplace with the dining area and kitchen. The kitchen is super functional with a built-in circular island for extra dining space that maximizes the square footage. The bathroom is oversized and luxurious, pampering both of the bedrooms.

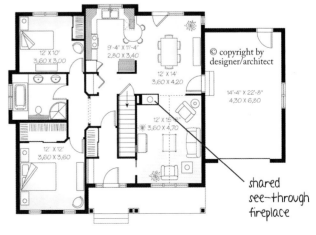

12' X 10'
3,60 X 3,00

9'-4" X 11'-4"
2,80 X 3,40

© copyright by
designer/architect

12' X 14'
3,60 X 4,20

14'-4" X 22'-8"
4,30 X 6,80

12' X 15'
3,60 X 4,70

12' X 12'
3,60 X 3,60

shared
see-through
fireplace

GORHAM

The charming Gorham stone cottage is appealing and comfortable. A centered fireplace in the wonderful family room offers warmth as well as a stunning focal point. Extra dining is available at the kitchen counter that is shared with the comfortable dining area, featuring handy outdoor access.

PLAN #C19-032D-0082

1022 square feet of living area
width: 30'   depth: 36'-4"
2 bedrooms, 1 bath
2" x 6" exterior walls
basement foundation standard;
crawl space, floating slab, or monolithic slab available for a fee

plenty of space for a sizable table

18' X 12'
5,40 X 3,60

10' X 10'
3,00 X 3,00

12' X 16'
3,60 X 4,80

12' X 12'
3,60 X 3,60

© copyright by designer/architect

HAVERHILL LANE

PLAN #C19-011D-0446

1076 square feet of living area
width: 25'-6"   depth: 41'-6"
2 bedrooms, 2½ baths
2" x 6" exterior walls
joisted crawl space foundation standard;
slab or basement available for a fee

Haverhill Lane will take you back in time to when homes had so much character! The welcoming wraparound covered porch leads to the dining/living area with a corner fireplace. The U-shaped kitchen has a powder room and laundry closet. Upstairs you'll discover two bedrooms, each with their own bath.

first floor
572 sq. ft.

second floor
504 sq. ft.

© copyright by
designer/architect

13/7" X 9/3"
(9' CLG.)

DINING /
LIVING
13/7" X 19/5"
(9' CLG.)

REF.

D/W

COVERED PORCH

VAULTED
BR. 2
10/7" X 10/3"

LINEN
STOR.

VAULTED
BR. 1
13/7" X 10/9"

tons of usable
outdoor space

BARATHAVEN
A large arched window below a charming gable roof is the focal point of this home's facade. A high 11' ceiling in the great room creates a spacious feel. The combination kitchen and breakfast room allow easier cleanup after mealtimes.

PLAN #C19-060D-0014
1021 square feet of living area
width: 38' depth: 32'
3 bedrooms, 2 baths
crawl space or slab foundation,
please specify when ordering

FOXPORT
A brick facade and a feature window add elegance to this narrow lot home. The vaulted living room enjoys a fireplace and opens to a U-shaped kitchen with a bayed breakfast area, snack bar, and built-in pantry.

PLAN #C19-007D-0107
1161 square feet of living area
width: 30' depth: 44'-4"
3 bedrooms, 2 baths
basement foundation

BARROW BAY
This home boasts plenty of open living spaces ideal for entertaining. A sunny bay window adds style and charm to the interior as well as the exterior of the home.

PLAN #C19-032D-0009
1191 square feet of living area
width: 31'-6" depth: 40'-2"
2 bedrooms, 1 bath
2" x 6" exterior walls
basement foundation standard; crawl space,
floating slab, or monolithic slab available for a fee

WINDINGPATH
This home's front and rear covered porches provide great spaces to relax with friends and family, while also extending the living space to the outdoors.

PLAN #C19-077D-0105
1100 square feet of living area
width: 31'-2" depth: 48'-6"
2 bedrooms, 2 baths
ICF exterior walls
slab foundation

156

PINEVIEW
This home has a pleasant covered porch entry. The kitchen, living room, and dining areas combine maximizing space. The bedrooms are near each other for convenience with small children.

PLAN #C19-001D-0018
988 square feet of living area
width: 50' depth: 30'
3 bedrooms, 1 bath
basement or crawl space foundation,
please specify when ordering

RIDGEWOOD
Handsome curb appeal has been created thanks to a triple-gable facade. An efficient U-shaped kitchen has a snack bar and a breakfast room open to the living room with bay window.

PLAN #C19-007D-0112
1062 square feet of living area
width: 42'-8" depth: 45'
3 bedrooms, 2 baths
basement foundation

SONA
A sleek, unique getaway home is ideal for a lot with a front view! The kitchen, living area, and screened porch all enjoy front views and benefit being lakefront. Two bedrooms are tucked in back for privacy and comfort.

PLAN #C19-126D-1150
600 square feet of living area
width: 30' depth: 20'
2 bedrooms, 1 bath
2" x 6" exterior walls
pilings foundation

SHERWOOD COVE
A cute, affordable home that doesn't lack curb appeal! A great starter or retirement home with open living/dining areas leading to a deck. The master bedroom has a walk-in closet.

PLAN #C19-051D-0889
967 square feet of living area
width: 40' depth: 44'
3 bedrooms, 1 bath
2" x 6" exterior walls
basement foundation standard;
crawl space or slab available for a fee

LOGAN HILL
A vaulted family room invites guests to relax and stay awhile as they enter the welcoming covered front entry. The kitchen and dining room combine for convenience at mealtimes. All bedrooms are located near each other for convenience.

PLAN #C19-087D-0016
1199 square feet of living area
width: 33' depth: 53'
3 bedrooms, 2 baths
slab foundation

PATTI PEAK
Rustic and modern style collide, forming this special home with tons of natural light, angled ceilings, and a refreshing personality. Spacious open living and dining rooms have easy kitchen access. Both bedrooms access the bath, making this layout effortless.

PLAN #C19-148D-0022
1013 square feet of living area
width: 46' depth: 38'
2 bedrooms, 1 bath
2" x 6" exterior walls
basement foundation

WHISTLER
A rustic modern masterpiece sure to brighten any neighborhood! An open-concept floor plan has one central area for dining, cooking, and gathering. Two bedrooms share a bath with washer/dryer space.

PLAN #C19-148D-0026
938 square feet of living area
width: 32' depth: 33'
2 bedrooms, 1 bath
2" x 6" exterior walls
basement foundation

ELLENWOOD
A fireplace flanked by sunny windows graces the family room. The delightful kitchen and cheerful breakfast area combine for a relaxing atmosphere with access onto the rear patio.

PLAN #C19-076D-0013
1177 square feet of living area
width: 51'-6" depth: 48'-3"
3 bedrooms, 2 baths
slab foundation

GREENBAY
The entry, with convenient stairs to the basement, leads to spacious living and dining rooms open to the kitchen. The master bedroom enjoys double entry doors, a walk-in closet, and a private bath with linen closet.

PLAN #C19-007D-0181
1140 square feet of living area
width: 38' depth: 52'-8"
3 bedrooms, 2 baths
basement, crawl space, or slab foundation,
please specify when ordering

MAPLE BROOK
A sleek stucco home perfect for the sunbelt region! A spacious covered back porch provides shaded outdoor space. Equipped with all the cooking necessities, the kitchen has a dining area and laundry room access, creating a hub of high function.

PLAN #C19-069D-0109
1013 square feet of living area
width: 36' depth: 41'
2 bedrooms, 2 baths
crawl space or slab foundation,
please specify when ordering

WOODSON
With a cozy den and study, this small home promises to have quiet, private spaces in addition to the open ones. Other great features include a bath/laundry room and walk-in closet in the bedroom.

PLAN #C19-141D-0117
815 square feet of living area
width: 32'-10" depth: 31'-5"
1 bedroom, 1½ baths
slab foundation

JENNY MANOR
A two-story foyer invites you into the great room with a two-story fireplace, bookshelves, and a window wall. Amenities galore in the kitchen including a 9' island with seating and dining area.

PLAN #C19-007D-0201
1153 square feet of living area
width: 37'-4" depth: 47'-8"
3 bedrooms, 2 baths
basement foundation

APARTMENT GARAGE DECOR IDEAS

Apartment garage living is a great solution to many family changes. Whether you have a child home from college or you have a live-in parent who requires some assistance but can do many tasks unsupervised, a garage apartment may be the perfect fit for your family's needs. But how do you make an apartment garage feel comfortable, cozy, and functional? The last thing you want it to feel like is, well…a garage.

To make apartment garage living feel like a home, special challenges need to be met. First, square footage has to be maximized to its fullest. Apartment garages are small, so every inch of the floor plan has to be accounted for when selecting and placing furniture. An oversized sofa or L-shaped sofa may be what you want, but once you get them in a small space, they may appear too monstrous. Carefully choose furniture pieces so they are multifunctional yet comfortable. Versatile furniture pieces include futons or sofa beds that offer additional sleeping space as well as seating when entertaining. Or, use an ottoman to double as a stool for seating and add a tray on top for easy additional table space that can be placed anywhere at anytime. Stacking tables also add function by using very little floor space, but they can be separated to provide extra tables near seating areas when entertaining. Multifunctional furniture pieces will give you the extra function without overcrowding the interior with too much furniture.

Another universal challenge with garage apartments is their lack of storage. Apartment garages aren't known for having spacious walk-in closets. In fact, the closets are often tiny. So get creative with adding storage. Purchase adjustable rods and add to the closets for extra rows of hanging space. Also, install pullout rods that can be extended in the bathroom for a handy place to hang a robe or towel.

If you have a hard time finding places for items like seasonal decorations or family mementos; use the space under the bed or sofa. Raise your bed with cement blocks and add a longer bed skirt to hide them. The extra height creates more storage space while creating an elegance to your bedroom or sleeping area.

Another stylish way to add storage is to find shelves that act as decoration but also offer functionality. Shelves provide a great spot for collectibles and keep the floor space open. Whether it's a shelf with towels in the bathroom, or a shelf with books above the bed, it's functional but provides architectural interest. Browse local flea markets or yard and estate sales for one-of-a-kind shelves that create a stylish focal point.

ACCESSORIES TO OPEN UP THE SPACE

Many apartment garages have open floor plans with all of the living spaces combined. In many ways, this is a plus because additional walls separating everything would only make the interior feel even smaller. But, with all spaces as one, sometimes separation visually needs to occur to make it function properly.

Try building or buying a screen to create privacy from the sleeping area to the living space. Or remove the screen to open up the space.

Also, use rugs to visually separate the interior. Try a bold pattern such as a stripe to act as a partition between the living space and the bedroom.

Mirrors give the illusion of a larger space, no matter its size. Placing mirrors across from windows also adds extra light, meaning less need for extra lamps.

Whatever your needs may be, an apartment garage is a great solution by creating additional living space that is private yet convenient to the main home. Use these inexpensive decorating tips for small spaces and make your garage apartment feel comfortable, cozy, and functional all at the same time.

APARTMENT GARAGES

Plan #C19-013D-0163 is found on page 180.

Apartment garages have taken on a whole new meaning for many families looking for flexibility today. Instead of packing up and moving when your home begins to shrink, why not stay put and build an apartment garage for the children home from college, house guests, or even the in-law no longer able to live entirely on their own? An apartment garage is the perfect solution! There are so many floor plan options, features, and architectural styles, you will have no problem finding an apartment garage that complements the architectural style of your existing home. Or, why not build an apartment garage as a vacation rental or a retirement getaway for yourself? The options are truly limitless!

CARLEY CANYON APARTMENT GARAGE

This stylish apartment garage sets itself apart from all of the others with its sleek exterior, no-nonsense style, and its open and bright welcoming interior. The galley kitchen is steps away from the open living area, with windows on every wall filling the space with an abundance of natural sunlight. A centrally located laundry closet is near both bedrooms and the full bathroom. This is truly luxury apartment living designed with today's love of modern style!

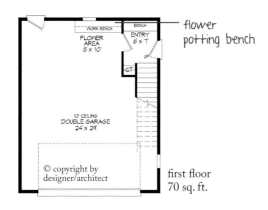

flower
potting bench

first floor
70 sq. ft.

WORK BENCH   BENCH
FLOWER
AREA
8' x 10'
ENTRY
6' x 7'

10' CEILING
DOUBLE GARAGE
24' x 29'

© copyright by
designer/architect

BEDROOM #2
12 x 11

BEDROOM #1
12 x 11

CLO

LNDRY

SHELVES

BATH
9 x 6

LIVING
14 x 18

KITCHEN
10 x 8

BALCONY

easy access to
stackable washer
and dryer

second floor
750 sq. ft.

PLAN #C19-142D-7500

820 square feet of living area
width: 25' depth: 34'
2 bedrooms, 1 bath
2" x 6" exterior walls
slab foundation

FRIDA APARTMENT GARAGE

This sleek, vaulted studio apartment is sure to turn heads, and is a great option to complement today's ever-so popular modern home design trend. The shed-style roof of the Frida apartment garage adds eye-catching curb appeal to the exterior. While the second floor studio enjoys a compact kitchen and built-in desk space, there is also a full bath with space for a stackable washer and dryer, plus a linen closet to optimize storage. Who said apartment garage living was boring?

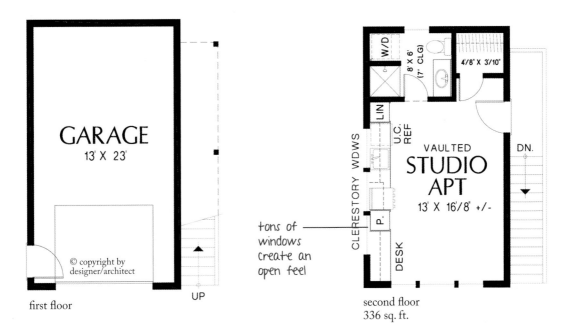

GARAGE
13' X 23'

© copyright by
designer/architect

first floor

UP

W/D

8' X 6'
(7' CLG)

4/8" X 3/10"

LIN

CLERESTORY WDWS

U.C.
REF

P.

DESK

VAULTED
STUDIO
APT
13' X 16/8' +/-

DN.

tons of
windows
create an
open feel

second floor
336 sq. ft.

PLAN #C19-012D-7506

336 square feet of living area
width: 17'-6"   depth: 24'
1 bedroom, 1 bath
2" x 6" exterior walls
slab foundation

JENSEN APARTMENT & RV GARAGE

Storage is literally at every turn in this two-bedroom apartment garage with space for multiple vehicles, including a recreation vehicle. A covered patio and half bath are found off the massive garage for convenience on the first floor. The second floor apartment features a kitchen with island seating for four people that overlooks the living area. Two spacious bedrooms, a bath, and tons of storage complete the space.

second floor
896 sq. ft.

tons of
storage

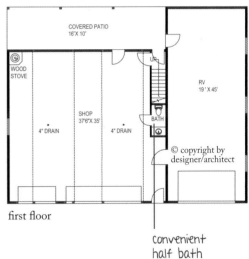

first floor

convenient
half bath

PLAN #C19-133D-7511

896 square feet of living area
width: 58'   depth: 46'
2 bedrooms, 1½ baths
slab foundation

BABETTE
APARTMENT
GARAGE

With an abundance of storage in each of the bedrooms and at the top of the stairs, living in the Babette apartment garage will not be difficult. The large living area enjoys a cozy fireplace and has plenty of space for a dining table. Each bedroom has a full bath nearby and its own walk-in closet. The U-shaped kitchen is compact yet efficient and is just steps from the main gathering spaces for ease.

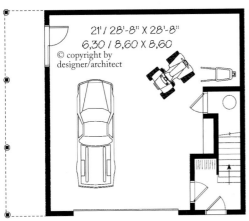

21' / 28'-8" X 28'-8"
6,30 / 8,60 X 8,60
© copyright by
designer/architect

first floor
128 sq. ft.

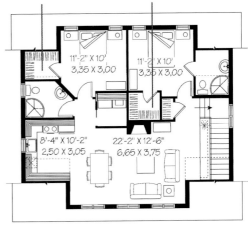

walk-in closets in both bedrooms

11'-2" X 10'
3,35 X 3,00

11'-2" X 10'
3,35 X 3,00

8'-4" X 10'-2"
2,50 X 3,05

22'-2" X 12'-6"
6,65 X 3,75

second floor
968 sq. ft.

PLAN #C19-113D-7505

1096 square feet of living area
width: 36'   depth: 30'
2 bedrooms, 2 baths
2" x 6" exterior walls
floating slab foundation standard;
monolithic slab available for a fee

KARIBOO APARTMENT GARAGE

Who said apartment garages have to be boring, or lack style? The Kariboo apartment garage is anything but! The modern and sleek exterior gives way to a 2-car garage on the first floor and an open and bright living space on the second floor, with panoramic views in every direction thanks to countless windows lining each and every wall. Two bedrooms share a bath to complete the floor plan. This style would allow you to take advantage of stunning mountain or coastal views in every direction.

so much
extra storage

balcony access
in three places

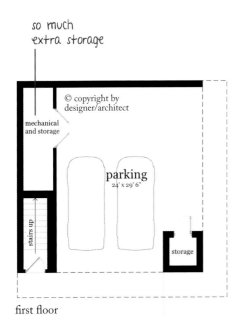

© copyright by
designer/architect

mechanical
and storage

stairs up

parking
24' x 29' 6"

storage

first floor

shower

closet

closet

bed 1
12' 1" x 11' 7"

w/d

bath

bed 2
11' 8" x 11' 7"

stairs down

dw

sink

stove

under-counter
refrigerators

living / dining
22' 4" x 17' 7"

balcony

second floor
930 sq. ft.

PLAN #C19-152D-0030

930 square feet of living area
110 bonus square feet
width: 35'   depth: 35'
2 bedrooms, 1 bath
2" x 6" exterior walls
slab foundation

KODY FARM

Rustic, with a rural style, this 4-car garage apartment has two covered carport areas and a tandem-style garage entry. The second floor has a spacious living room with fireplace, a U-shaped kitchen, two bedrooms with walk-in closets and their own baths, plus a laundry room. Small, cozy comfort!

PLAN #C19-133D-7509

1092 square feet of living area
width: 36'   depth: 50'
2 bedrooms, 2 baths
slab foundation

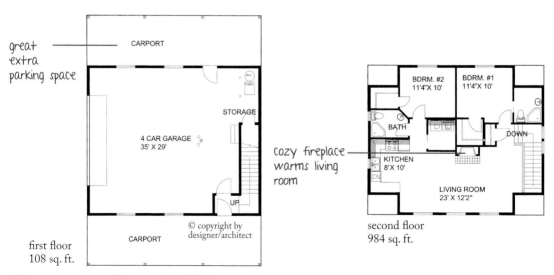

great extra parking space

CARPORT

STORAGE

4 CAR GARAGE
35' X 29'

UP

CARPORT

© copyright by designer/architect

first floor
108 sq. ft.

cozy fireplace warms living room

BDRM. #2
11'4"X 10'

BDRM. #1
11'4"X 10'

BATH

DOWN

KITCHEN
8'X 10'

LIVING ROOM
23' X 12'2"

second floor
984 sq. ft.

JUSTINE CREEK

PLAN #C19-002D-7526

566 square feet of living area
width: 28' depth: 24'
studio, 1 bath
floating slab foundation
material list/instructions included

The charming dormers of the Justine Creek apartment garage add major curb appeal to this design. The second floor features a comfortable studio apartment with an open living area, dormer windows adding character, a corner kitchen, a walk-in closet, and a full bath.

Garage
23'-5" x 23-4"

© copyright by
designer/architect

first floor

Dn

Studio
18'-2" x 18-4"

Sloped Clg

R

dormers add
style inside
and out

second floor
566 sq. ft.

PARKHILL

The Parkhill is disguised as a home but in reality offers stylish apartment garage living. The living room with dining area has a balcony deck with sliding glass door access. The kitchen has a breakfast bar, an oval window above the sink, and plenty of cabinets. The master bedroom has a walk-in closet and large window. Laundry and storage closets and mechanical space are found on the first floor.

PLAN #C19-007D-0070

929 square feet of living area
width: 31'   depth: 35'
2 bedrooms, 1 bath
slab foundation

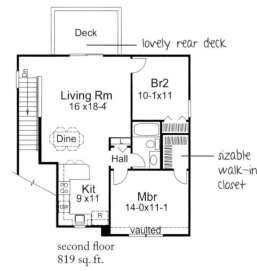

storage and laundry closet in the garage

HW F
Stor.
W
D
Up
Entry

Patio

Garage
23-4'x29-4'

© copyright by designer/architect

first floor
110 sq. ft.

Porch

Deck

lovely rear deck

Living Rm
16 x18-4

Dine

Kit
9 x11

DW

Hall

Br2
10-1x11

sizable walk-in closet

Mbr
14-0x11-1

R

vaulted

second floor
819 sq. ft.

GLENWOOD

PLAN #C19-007D-0040

632 square feet of living area
width: 28'   depth: 26'
1 bedroom, 1 bath
slab foundation

The covered porch leads to a vaulted entry featuring a staircase with an arched window, a coat closet, and access to the garage and laundry area. Upstairs you'll find a cozy vaulted living room with fireplace, a large arched window, and a handy pass-through to the kitchen. There's also a luxurious bath with a garden tub and arched window above.

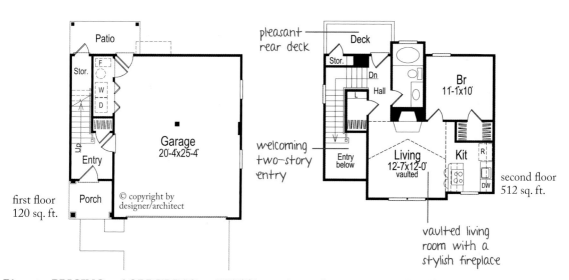

pleasant rear deck

Deck

welcoming two-story entry

vaulted living room with a stylish fireplace

Patio

Stor.

F
W
D

Up

Entry

Porch

Garage
20-4x25-4'

© copyright by
designer/architect

first floor
120 sq. ft.

Stor.

Dn

Hall

L

Br
11-1x10'

Entry
below

Living
12-7x12-0'
vaulted

Kit

R

DW

second floor
512 sq. ft.

DABNEY

Large rooms offer comfortable living in the Dabney apartment garage. With a second floor laundry room, ample cabinets, and sliding doors to an outdoor deck, this two-bedroom apartment garage is comfortable and inviting to all those who stay there.

PLAN #C19-002D-7529

1040 square feet of living area
width: 40'   depth: 26'
2 bedrooms, 1 bath
floating slab foundation
material list included

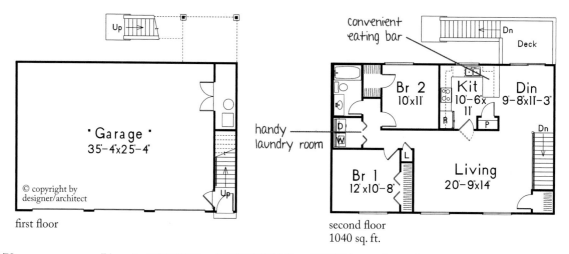

convenient eating bar

handy laundry room

Up

Garage
35'-4"x25'-4"

© copyright by designer/architect

first floor

Dn

Deck

Br 2
10'x11'

Kit
10'-6"x
11'

Din
9'-8"x11'-3"

Br 1
12'x10'-8"

Living
20'-9"x14'

Dn

second floor
1040 sq. ft.

PARK HOUSE

PLAN #C19-007D-0145

1005 square feet of living area
width: 40' depth: 38'
2 bedrooms, 1½ baths
slab foundation

A unique three-car garage with a rear apartment. This two-story apartment is disguised with a one-story facade featuring triple garage doors and a shed roof dormer. The side porch leads to an entry hall, a living room with fireplace and patio access, a U-shaped kitchen, a powder room, and a staircase to the second floor. The second floor is comprised of two bedrooms and a bath.

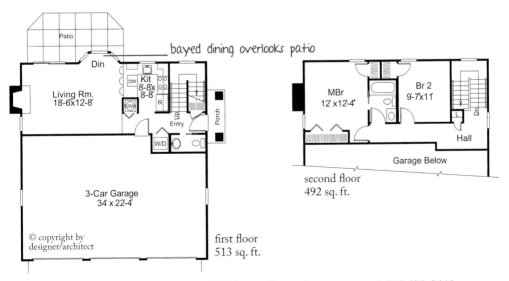

STONETRAIL

The living room has a bayed dining area, a separate entry with garage access, and a staircase to the second floor. An L-shaped kitchen has a linen closet nearby. The second floor has a bedroom with walk-in closet. A handy RV garage is also an asset.

PLAN #C19-007D-0189
713 square feet of living area
width: 39'-4"   depth: 42'-4"
1 bedroom, 1½ baths
slab foundation

SANDON

The garage has space for a handy washer/dryer. Upstairs the second floor has a vaulted family room between the kitchen and bedroom. There is plenty of storage throughout, including built-in shelves, a closet, and a pantry.

PLAN #C19-013D-0163
838 square feet of living area
width: 42'   depth: 24'
1 bedroom, 1 bath
slab foundation standard;
basement or crawl space available for a fee

PLATEAU PEAK

The beamed and vaulted great room, breakfast area, and kitchen are the main focal point of this studio apartment. A quiet bedroom and full bath complete the interior and offer great comfort.

PLAN #C19-142D-7529
780 square feet of living area
width: 30'-5"   depth: 40'
1 bedroom, 1 bath
slab foundation

BROCK

This two-car apartment garage enjoys a comfortable living space, including a great room, a sizable dining area, and a kitchen with a utility room steps away. The Brock apartment garage provides carefree, easy living.

PLAN #C19-059D-7514
728 square feet of living area
width: 31'   depth: 26'
1 bedroom, 1 bath
footing and foundation wall

PALMERHILL
This stylish apartment garage includes plenty of storage, including built-in shelves and a desk in the living area. There is a functional U-shaped kitchen and a bedroom and bath combo, including space for a washer and dryer.

PLAN #C19-012D-7501
633 square feet of living area
width: 28' depth: 26'
1 bedroom, 1 bath
2" x 6" exterior walls
slab foundation

PINEWOOD
The vaulted living room has a kitchenette, fireplace, and a separate entry with a closet. The staircase leads to a second-floor bedroom with a bath, a walk-in closet, and a unique opening with louvered doors that can overlook the living room below.

PLAN #C19-007D-0191
641 square feet of living area
width: 28' depth: 31'
1 bedroom, 1½ baths
slab foundation

KALINDA
This apartment garage has two garage bays and a look that easily complements many styles of homes. The loft has a roomy kitchen and dining area, as well as a private side entrance.

PLAN #C19-002D-7528
576 square feet of living area
width: 24' depth: 24'
1 bedroom, 1 bath
floating slab foundation
material list/instructions included

CARLYN
Stylish facade with a Country French influence looks great with many styles of homes being built today. Open studio space with an L-shaped kitchen has a private bedroom down a hall.

PLAN #C19-098D-7502
540 square feet of living area
width: 40' depth: 24'
1 bedroom, 1 bath
slab foundation

LIDA
Stately columns create a sophisticated exterior appearance loaded with curb appeal. The spacious living/dining area has a box-bay window for indoor character. The kitchen has double French doors to a second-floor deck.

PLAN #C19-071D-0246
755 square feet of living area
width: 35' depth: 30'
1 bedroom, 1 bath
2" x 6" exterior walls
slab foundation

QUAIL VALLEY
Both bedrooms have access to their own private balcony and share a bath. There is a spacious living area with a large kitchen and dining space. A central washer/dryer closet is accessible from anywhere, making chore time a breeze.

PLAN #C19-113D-7500
992 square feet of living area
width: 28' depth: 32'
2 bedrooms, 1^1/$_2$ baths
2" x 6" exterior walls
floating slab foundation standard;
monolithic slab available for a fee

Blueprint PRICING and ORDERING + VISIT houseplansandmore.com + 1-800-373-2646

SPENCER PARK
This western-style apartment garage has an open living area that is spacious and functional. Plus, it even includes space for the utilities right off the kitchen for utmost convenience.

PLAN #C19-002D-7519
784 square feet of living area
width: 28' depth: 28'
1 bedroom, 1 bath
floating slab foundation
material list/instructions included

HELLER
So much curb appeal with this two-car apartment garage! Dining, cooking, and living spaces combine to form a large area with an island overlooking it all. A private bedroom is near a bath for ease.

PLAN #C19-126D-1057
683 square feet of living area
width: 36' depth: 26'
1 bedroom, 1 bath
2" x 6" exterior walls
basement foundation

BUNGALOW
Step into a private foyer and go either straight upstairs to the studio apartment or proceed to the 2-car garage. The simple second floor layout includes a vaulted living area with a bath and walk-in closet.

PLAN #C19-162D-6001
510 square feet of living area
width: 22'   depth: 29'
1 bedroom, 1 bath
2" x 6" exterior walls
slab foundation

NEWTON PARK
The front entrance leads to an entry that accesses both the garage and the apartment. Located behind the garage is the perfect room for an office or workshop, and it has sliding glass doors to a rear patio so getting some fresh air is easy.

PLAN #C19-007D-0188
656 square feet of living area
width: 17'   depth: 34'
studio, 1 bath
slab foundation

Blueprint PRICING and ORDERING + VISIT houseplansandmore.com + 1-800-373-2646

HOBART
This two-car apartment garage has ample vehicle space plus an apartment with a kitchen, living and dining areas, a full bath, and a separate bedroom for plenty of privacy.

PLAN #C19-002D-7510
746 square feet of living area
width: 28'   depth: 26'
1 bedroom, 1 bath
floating slab foundation
material list/instructions included

LAYCIE
This three-car apartment garage offers plenty of space for vehicles plus the perfect sitting area near the kitchen/dining space, including an attractive window seat as a charming focal point.

PLAN #C19-059D-7504
949 square feet of living area
width: 40'   depth: 27'
1 bedroom, 1 bath
footing and foundation wall

WHITNEY HILL
GARAGE WITH LOFT

The Whitney Hill workshop garage is a convenient two-car garage with a workshop and a partial loft space above, ideal for storage. A large workshop on the main floor has a 6' x 6'-8" double door, allowing easy entry into the space when working on mechanics or larger items or machinery. The addition of the partial loft offers extra storage, always appreciated by hobby enthusiasts.

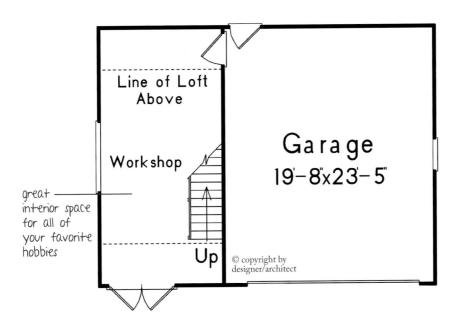

Line of Loft Above

Workshop

great interior space for all of your favorite hobbies

Up

Garage
19'-8"x23'-5"

© copyright by
designer/architect

PLAN #C19-002D-6002

width: 32'   depth: 24'
building height: 20'-2"
floating slab foundation
material list/instructions included

BIGLEY GARAGE WITH LOFT

This two-car garage is a wonderful structure that adds so much character to any backyard or lot. Not only is it an attractive way to house additional vehicles, yard equipment, and other items, it has a classic look that looks great with many architectural styles of homes. If you need an additional garage or storage spot, then look no further than the charming Bigley garage with loft above.

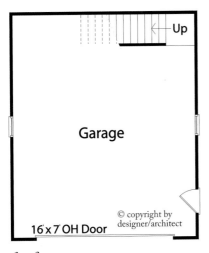

Up

Garage

16 x 7' OH Door

© copyright by
designer/architect

first floor

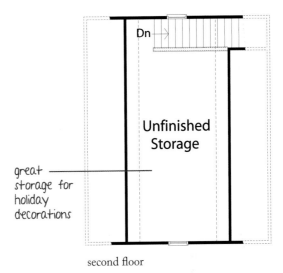

Dn

Unfinished
Storage

great
storage for
holiday
decorations

second floor

PLAN #C19-059D-6107

width: 22'   depth: 26'
building height: 23'-8"
footing and foundation wall

LIBBY COVE GARAGE WITH LOFT

This two-car garage with large loft above has so much to offer! Off the garage is a rear covered porch for enjoying a much-appreciated shaded outdoor space. The second-floor loft has multiple windows creating a simple Craftsman appearance to the exterior. There is the option to add a half bath, and there is double door access onto a huge deck with a spiral staircase leading to the ground floor. An ultra private third-floor deck is the perfect private sunning spot.

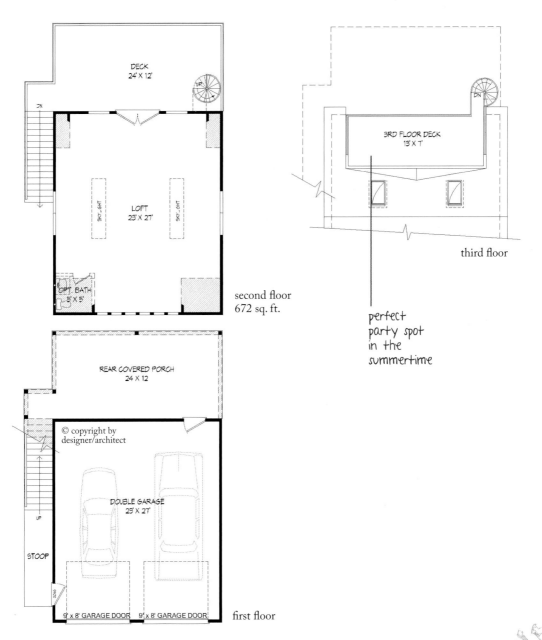

DECK
24' X 12'

DN

LOFT
23' X 27'

SKY. GHT

SKY. GHT

OPT. BATH
5' X 5'

second floor
672 sq. ft.

3RD FLOOR DECK
13' X 7'

DN

third floor

perfect
party spot
in the
summertime

REAR COVERED PORCH
24 X 12

© copyright by
designer/architect

DOUBLE GARAGE
23' X 27'

UP

STOOP

9' x 8' GARAGE DOOR   9' x 8' GARAGE DOOR

first floor

PLAN #C19-142D-6135

672 square feet of living area
width: 28'   depth: 40'
building height: 26'-7"
slab foundation

SOMMERTON

The Sommerton garage has a shingle-style roof and a large dormer window, adding style to the exterior of this two-car garage structure with a workshop and storage. A quaint covered front porch offers a great place for taking a break from a tedious project. The workshop includes ladder access to the storage loft above.

PLAN #C19-117D-6000

1058 square feet of living area
width: 30'   depth: 25'
building height: 24'
2" x 6" exterior walls
slab foundation

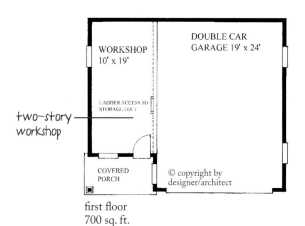

two-story workshop

WORKSHOP 10' x 19'

DOUBLE CAR GARAGE 19' x 24'

LADDER ACCESS TO STORAGE LOFT

COVERED PORCH

© copyright by designer/architect

first floor
700 sq. ft.

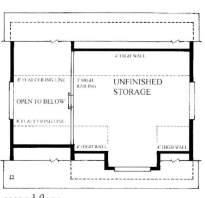

4' HIGH WALL

8' FLAT CEILING LINE

3' HIGH RAILING

UNFINISHED STORAGE

OPEN TO BELOW

8' FLAT CEILING LINE

4' HIGH WALL

4' HIGH WALL

second floor
358 sq. ft.

LANELLE

PLAN #C19-059D-6013

width: 32'   depth: 26'
building height: 26'
footing and foundation wall

Undeniable charm plays a huge part in the style of the Lanelle two-car garage with a trio of dormer windows. The windows fill the unfinished storage area with plenty of natural light, making it a cheerful workshop or home office space.

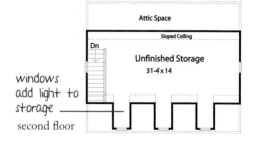

windows add light to storage

second floor

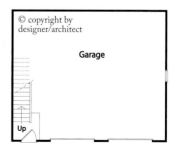

first floor

MERAMEC

A four-car garage with so much more! The first floor includes a pool bath with an oversized walk-in shower. There are also two large storage spaces; one perfect for yard equipment and the other ideal as a workshop. The second-floor loft has a wet bar and a completely open space for creating an entertaining spot, man cave, or a studio apartment.

PLAN #C19-142D-7516

1064 square feet of living area
width: 40'   depth: 37'
1 bath
building height: 24'-8"
slab foundation

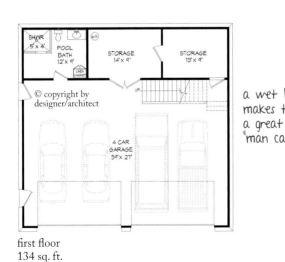

SHWR 5' x 4'

POOL BATH 12' x 9'

LINEN CABINET

STORAGE 14' x 9'

STORAGE 13' x 9'

© copyright by designer/architect

UP

4 CAR GARAGE 39' x 27'

first floor
134 sq. ft.

a wet bar makes this a great "man cave"

HVAC / MECH

ATTIC

WET BAR

LOFT 39' x 29'

DN

second floor
930 sq. ft.

HOMESTEAD

PLAN #C19-117D-6001

width: 24'   depth: 35'
building height: 23'
2" x 6" exterior walls
slab foundation

The lovely Homestead rustic Craftsman two-car garage features an open two-story entry and workshop space with a coat closet. The open second floor is perfect for storage, a spacious art studio, or hobby room, and it has three large windows filling the space with plenty of natural sunlight.

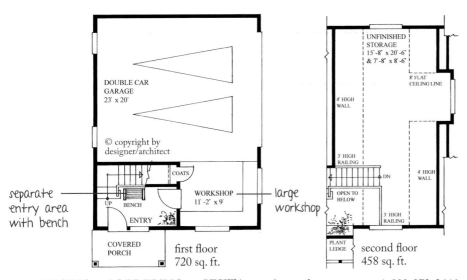

DOUBLE CAR GARAGE 23' x 20'

© copyright by designer/architect

separate entry area with bench

COATS

UP   BENCH

ENTRY

COVERED PORCH

WORKSHOP 11'-2" x 9'

large workshop

first floor 720 sq. ft.

UNFINISHED STORAGE 15'-8" x 20'-6" & 7'-8" x 8'-6"

8' FLAT CEILING LINE

4' HIGH WALL

3' HIGH RAILING

OPEN TO BELOW

DN

4' HIGH WALL

3' HIGH RAILING

PLANT LEDGE

second floor 458 sq. ft.

The Hector garage with loft features space for three vehicles and has a rustic Craftsman-influenced facade, great with many of today's home designs. The second-floor loft space includes a cozy woodstove for added warmth when working on projects in the cooler months of the year.

PLAN #C19-126D-1056

384 square feet of living area
width: 30'   depth: 24'
building height: 23'
2" x 6" exterior walls
basement foundation

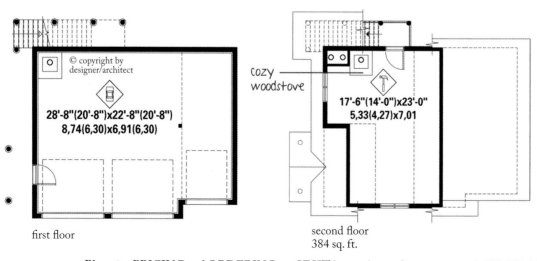

© copyright by designer/architect

28'-8"(20'-8")x22'-8"(20'-8")
8,74(6,30)x6,91(6,30)

first floor

cozy woodstove

17'-6"(14'-0")x23'-0"
5,33(4,27)x7,01

second floor
384 sq. ft.

SAVANNA

PLAN #C19-142D-7510

1027 square feet of living area
width: 24'-10"   depth: 32'-10"
building height: 27'-8"
1 bath
slab foundation

A garage with many purposes! The Savanna single-car garage has a large office on the first floor in addition to a full bath with a walk-in shower. Plenty of additional storage is found near the garage, making this space also ideal as a workshop. The second floor is an open recreation room space, perfect as a man cave or a family game room.

STORAGE
15' X 8'

SH/WR
4' X 3'

3/4
BATH

DN

SINGLE
GARAGE
12' X 23'

OFFICE
11' X 19'

great
private
home
office

© copyright by
designer/architect

9'x8' GARAGE DOOR

first floor
358 sq. ft.

DN

REC ROOM
22' X 27'

large
flex
space

second floor
669 sq. ft.

MAYER LANE

The charming style of the Mayer Lane two-car loft garage is so appealing it will be a welcome addition to any backyard and also looks great with many architectural styles of homes. Windows on all four walls of the second-floor attic add sunlight to the interior, making it a very functional space that's cheerful enough for a home office.

PLAN #C19-136D-6001

590 square feet
width: 26'   depth: 28'
building height: 25'-3"
slab foundation

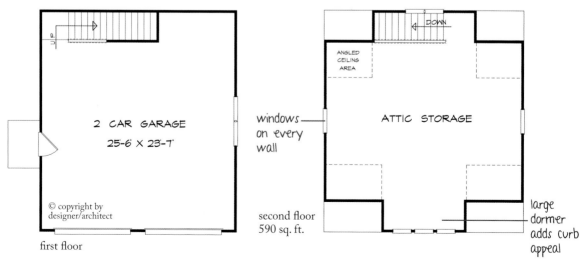

UP

2 CAR GARAGE
25-6 X 23-7

© copyright by
designer/architect

first floor

DOWN

ANGLED
CEILING
AREA

windows
on every
wall

ATTIC STORAGE

second floor
590 sq. ft.

large
dormer
adds curb
appeal

WATERVILLE

PLAN #C19-012D-7500

1179 square feet
width: 48'   depth: 36'
1 bath
building height: 26'
2" x 6" exterior walls
slab foundation

The Waterville garage and loft offers three garage bays, a large storage area, and a full bath on the first floor. The vaulted second floor bonus room would make an ideal home office or hobby area and includes an outdoor balcony to get a much needed break and some fresh air every now and then.

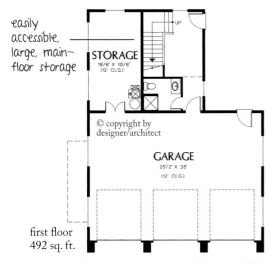

easily accessible, large, main-floor storage

STORAGE
19/6" X 10/6"
(12' CLG.)

© copyright by designer/architect

GARAGE
25/2" X 35'
(12' CLG.)

first floor
492 sq. ft.

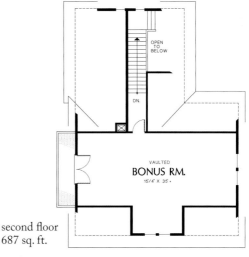

OPEN TO BELOW

DN.

VAULTED
BONUS RM.
15/4" X 35'±

second floor
687 sq. ft.

LORA
A solid brick exterior makes a lasting impression with this three-car garage with roomy loft above. Wouldn't a hobby or craft room be ideal in this attractive garage?

PLAN #C19-108D-6001
749 square feet
width: 38'   depth: 24'
building height: 24'-8"
slab foundation standard;
basement or crawl space available for a fee

KARISMA
Sit in the shade of the covered porch and enjoy this perfect entertaining or relaxing spot. Two large storage spaces on the second floor can also convert to living spaces, such as a home office or artist's studio.

PLAN #C19-108D-6000
664 square feet
width: 38'   depth: 24'
building height: 24'-8"
slab foundation standard;
basement or crawl space available for a fee

LANIKA
This two-car garage has a combination of brick veneer and siding to create an exterior with country-style curb appeal. The second-floor unfinished storage area can easily be converted to a secluded home office.

PLAN #C19-059D-6014
377 square feet
width: 24'   depth: 30'-4"
building height: 25'
footing and foundation wall

TARYN
The perfect two-car garage with loft option for any classic country-, Traditional-, or Cape Cod-style home. Twin dormers add additional sunlight to the second-story loft and an undeniable charm all their own.

PLAN #C19-002D-6001
width: 28'   depth: 24'
building height: 21'
floating slab or slab foundation,
please specify when ordering
material list/instructions included

WHITLEY PARK

This two-car garage is a fantastic choice if you're looking for a garage with storage featuring a Gambrel or barn-style roof. The exterior really suits a farm or country setting perfectly.

PLAN #C19-002D-6000

width: 22'   depth: 26'
building height: 20'-7"
floating slab foundation
material list/instructions included

GENESIS

This three-car garage with loft embodies country charm to the fullest with its unique dormers and Gambrel barn-style cedar-shingle roof design. The loft makes a perfect workshop or storage area, and there's a functional workbench in the garage.

PLAN #C19-107D-6003

includes 3 sizes:
26' x 24'   30' x 24'   36' x 24'
building height: 21'
slab or floating slab foundation,
please specify when ordering
material list/instructions included

Blueprint PRICING and ORDERING + VISIT houseplansandmore.com + 1-800-373-2646

NOLAND FARM

This barn-inspired two-car garage with loft above includes a functional and attractive second-floor double door for getting items down using a pulley system.

PLAN #C19-142D-7552

617 square feet
width: 28'   depth: 36'
building height: 25'-1"
2" x 6" exterior walls
slab foundation

RICHERT

This two-car garage makes a great addition to any lot that features a country-style barn or shed. It includes two large garage bays and storage overhead, all with a clean, simple style.

PLAN #C19-059D-6076

171 square feet
width: 34'   depth: 27'
building height: 24'
footing and foundation wall

DANICA LANE
This two-car garage has an attached RV garage for housing all of your vehicles safely and securely in one place. There's a second-floor loft space, and the first floor has a full bath and a place for a washer and dryer.

PLAN #C19-012D-6008
734 square feet of living area
width: 55'   depth: 50'
building height: 30'
2" x 6" exterior walls
slab foundation

BARROW
This garage has two stalls and an impressive stone facade creating curb appeal. Located upstairs is a spacious loft ideal as an office or for extra storage, or finish it into a small apartment. Several windows add natural light to both floors.

PLAN #C19-051D-0944
3195 square feet
width: 50'   depth: 42'
1/2 bath
building height: 30'-8"
2" x 6" exterior walls
slab foundation

PRIMA
This two-car garage has a second-floor loft that provides extra storage, while the clerestory window brightens the interior, eliminating the need and expense of installing electricity if you desire.

PLAN #C19-002D-6015
width: 26'   depth: 24'
building height: 20'
floating slab foundation
material list/instructions included

ANDREWS
This attractive two-car garage with loft has an interior staircase for accessing the second floor easily, and its classic good looks will complement many architectural styles.

PLAN #C19-142D-6102
444 square feet of living area
width: 24'   depth: 30'
building height: 21'-1"
slab foundation

TIARA
Classic country-style two-car garage has a staircase leading to the storage space overhead and is an ideal design for keeping your home uncluttered and organized.

PLAN #C19-002D-6039
width: 28'   depth: 24'
building height: 21'
floating slab foundation
material list included

RURALSPRING
Two 9' x 8' overhead garage doors in addition to an attractive cupola and gables are all appealing features of this two-car garage. The second-floor loft has four windows and space for any function you need.

PLAN #C19-059D-6010
width: 24'   depth: 30'
building height: 25'
footing and foundation wall

MOTORWORKS
A stylish two-car garage on the main floor with storage or game room space on the second floor. Make this your teenager's spot to retreat or a man cave game room for boy's poker night.

PLAN #C19-158D-7500
1075 square feet of living area
width: 38'-4"   depth: 51'-1"
building height: 25'-9"
concrete block or slab foundation, please specify when ordering

NAPLES SHORE
The Naples Shore two-car garage with studio loft space above has a unique slant roof that goes from 6' to 11' on the second floor, creating quite a dramatic space for an art studio or inspired office.

PLAN #C19-142D-6116
720 square feet of living area
width: 30'   depth: 24'
building height: 21'-5"
2" x 6" exterior walls
slab foundation

BEFORE BUILDING A SHED OR SMALL STRUCTURE

Building a shed or another small structure can be a simple project if the proper planning and guidelines are followed. Now more often than ever, people are turning to do-it-yourself projects as a way of adding additional storage, creating a place to enjoy hobbies or pastimes, or providing an entertainment or relaxation space, or even a home office. Why not build a shed or smaller structure to satisfy your specific needs?

A shed or other small structure, such as a studio, guest quarters, home office, or workshop, can potentially increase the value of your property while maintaining a well-organized home with the space you originally started with. Plus, the additional space will allow your household to run smoother. Maybe your family needs a workshop, or perhaps you need a utility shed for yard or garden equipment. Whatever your needs, there are hundreds of great sheds and other smaller structures designed to provide the perfect function you seem to be missing with your current home situation.

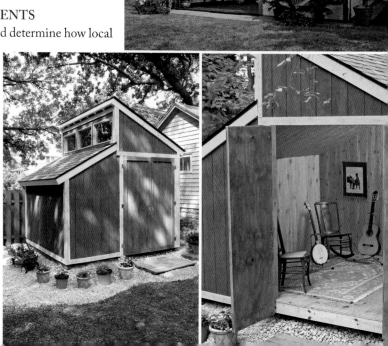

Here are some important factors to consider when constructing projects such as these to build on your existing lot. Before selecting a plan, review this checklist of design information you should gather before you make a final decision.

LOCAL BUILDING REQUIREMENTS
Visit your local building department and determine how local building codes and zoning ordinances will influence your project. Are you able to build a separate structure from your existing home? Are there height and size restrictions?

DEED RESTRICTIONS
Are there conditions in your property deed that restrict the type and location of an additional structure? Are you planning to place your shed or building on property controlled by an existing easement or utility access?

CLIMATIC FACTORS

Evaluate the micro-climate of your intended structure location. Micro-climate includes the shading effects of trees and shrubs, the angle of the sun in relation to nearby landscaping during different seasons, soil drainage conditions, and prevailing wind and temperature conditions. Remember, an enclosed shed without temperature regulation needs to be protected from the sun in the summer and exposed to any available sunlight in the winter, otherwise it will be impossible to use due to its comfort level.

OVERALL FUNCTION

Remember, the structure you intend to build should not only be functional, but should be an attractive addition to your yard. It can make a wonderful place for a gardener to house their tools and supplies, or create a workshop or hobby area perfectly designed for you and your needs. Adding storage shelves, electricity, and other amenities can only make your shed more personalized and functional to your needs. Always keep in mind the architectural style of your home on the land and do your best to complement your new structure to your existing home for a seamless and thoughtful finished look.

CHOOSING LUMBER FOR YOUR SHED

It is also important to think about what kind of lumber best suits your shed or structure. Consider both the positive and negative attributes of the lumber types listed below. Below is a concise guide to some common softwood lumber species used in construction. As you will see, each type of wood has its own good and bad qualities. You may make your decision based on your region of the country, the wood most commonly used in your area, or its durability. Or, perhaps you have a deck or other structure in your backyard already built with a specific type of wood. You may decide to use the same type for consistency.

- Cedar, Western Red - Popular for the durability and decay-resistance of its heartwood.
- Cypress - Cypress resists decay, is an attractive reddish coloration, and holds paint well.
- Douglas Fir, Larch - Douglas fir has great strength and is used best in the framing of your shed, especially in the floor joist members.
- Pines - Numerous pine species have excellent workability but are often pressure-treated for use in exterior construction.
- Southern Pine - Unlike the soft pines described above, southern pines possess strength but are only moderately decay- and warp-resistant.
- Poplar - Poplar has moderate strength and resists decay and warping.
- Redwood - A premium construction material because of its durability, resistance to decay, and beautiful natural brownish-red coloration.

A shed, studio, or other structure will not only provide necessary shelter and storage space, it can potentially increase the value of your home, making it a worthwhile addition, financially as well as for better function. Browse through our stylish sheds and other great small structures and find the perfect design for your specific needs.

SMALL
STRUCTURES
& SHEDS

Plan #C19-117D-6002 found on page 208.

All types of small structures can provide storage flexibility, ways to create additional income, or extra square footage to create better function in your existing home and life. Architects and designers now more than ever understand the needs of homeowners and are designing amazing small structures of all kinds that enhance your ability to relax, help you create space for hobbies, rid you of clutter, provide a productive work environment, or allow you to create comfortable spaces for loved ones or possibly renters. The options are endless when creating a space that is comfortable, fulfilling, and possibly even profitable. Whatever it is that you are searching for, there is a small structure perfect for you.

PASCAL
MODERN DWELLING

With its playful slant shed roof and modern style, the Pascal small dwelling is a sight to behold. Step onto the large porch and enter into a living area that enjoys plenty of sunshine through the multiple sliding glass doors. A small kitchen and a full bath offer complete comfort and could also create the potential for this to be a highly sought-after rental or vacation property, creating extra income.

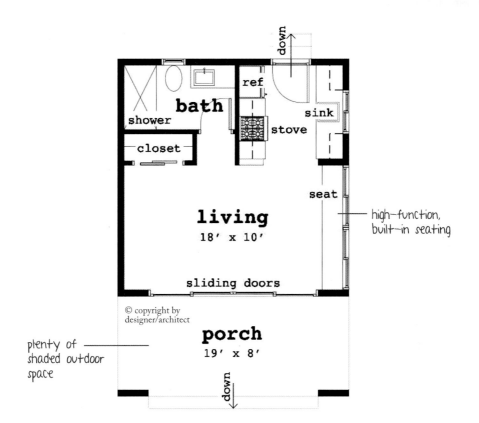

down

ref

bath

shower

sink

closet

stove

seat

high-function,
built-in seating

living

18' x 10'

sliding doors

© copyright by
designer/architect

plenty of
shaded outdoor
space

porch

19' x 8'

down

PLAN #C19-152D-0079

361 square feet of living area
width: 19'   depth: 27'
building height: 14'
1 bedroom, 1 bath
2" x 6" exterior walls
slab foundation

ROGERS RV GARAGE & WORKSHOP

The Rogers RV garage and workshop could be the perfect combination of fun and function for a retiree or hobby enthusiast! Store your recreational vehicle when not in use, and also enjoy tinkering with your favorite hobbies in an organized, designated place you can call your own. The workshop offers a tremendous amount of counterspace that wraps the entire space, perfect for organizing auto parts or hobby supplies.

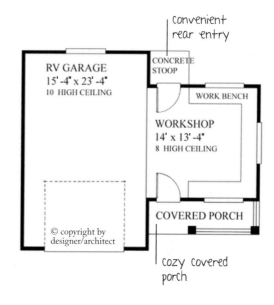

convenient
rear entry

RV GARAGE
15'-4" x 23'-4"
10 HIGH CEILING

CONCRETE
STOOP

WORK BENCH

WORKSHOP
14' x 13'-4"
8 HIGH CEILING

© copyright by
designer/architect

COVERED PORCH

cozy covered
porch

PLAN #C19-117D-6002

580 square feet of living area
width: 30'   depth: 24'
building height: 19'-6"
slab foundation

MANGO COVE
GUEST QUARTERS

Your guests may never want to leave this modern and inviting space! Tall ceilings, expansive windows, and a sleek interior with a full bath makes Mango Cove a tranquil and comfortable place for guests, visiting family members, a live-in parent, or an older child home from college. Just imagine if you have great views to complete the experience!

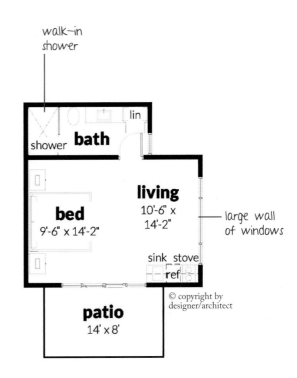

walk-in shower

shower **bath** lin

living
10'-6" x
14'-2"

bed
9'-6" x 14'-2"

large wall
of windows

sink stove
ref

© copyright by
designer/architect

patio
14' x 8'

PLAN #C19-162D-7504

405 square feet of living area
width: 21'   depth: 21'
1 bedroom, 1 bath
2" x 6" exterior walls
slab foundation

CASSELL CLUBHOUSE

Build your very own clubhouse and create a special place where the whole family can relax and enjoy time together! The billiard room easily becomes a game hub for all of your family's favorite activities. It connects to a rear covered porch, perfect for a barbecue grill. There are also large men's and women's bathrooms, featuring multiple toilets and showers, making this a great option poolside or as an entertaining space.

PLAN #C19-075D-7506

691 square feet of living area
width: 35'-5"   depth: 27'
2 baths
slab foundation

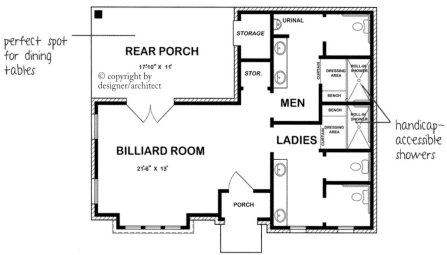

perfect spot for dining tables

REAR PORCH
17'10" X 11'
© copyright by designer/architect

STORAGE

URINAL

STOR.

MEN

LADIES

DRESSING AREA

ROLL-IN SHOWER

BENCH

BENCH

DRESSING AREA

ROLL-IN SHOWER

CURTAIN

CURTAIN

handicap-accessible showers

BILLIARD ROOM
21'-6" X 13'

PORCH

MARISELA GAME ROOM

PLAN #C19-009D-7542

780 square feet of living area
width: 28'   depth: 37'-9"
1 bath
slab foundation

The front covered patio is perfect for a hot tub or lounge area and accesses a sauna and full bath. The open room is designed for billiards or parties and has a corner fireplace, a 10' walk-in bar with storage, and space for darts, a jukebox, a popcorn machine, or pinball machine, making this a hub for family fun!

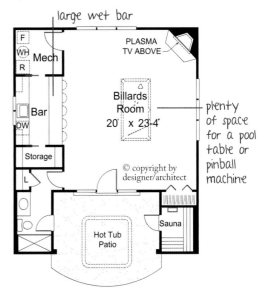

large wet bar

F
WH   Mech
R

PLASMA
TV ABOVE

Bar

DW

Billards
Room
20' x 23-4"

Storage

plenty
of space
for a pool
table or
pinball
machine

L

© copyright by
designer/architect

Hot Tub
Patio

Sauna

COCONUT OFFICE STUDIO

The tiny modern structure called Coconut is so attractive it would make working from home a complete joy and almost feel like a vacation! With its tall soaring ceilings, large windows, and built-in corner desk, this atmosphere would provide a place for creative thoughts to easily come to fruition all day long.

PLAN #C19-162D-7501

99 square feet of living area
width: 10'   depth: 11'
building height: 12'
2" x 6" exterior walls
slab foundation

seat

living
8'-2" x 9'

desk

efficient built-in desk

SOONER FIREPLACE

PLAN #C19-162D-7500

96 square feet of living area
width: 16'   depth: 10'
building height: 12'
slab foundation

This modern fireplace shelter would be a fun addition to any yard or pool area. Especially ideal in cooler climates, this structure has a covered porch and an interior featuring a large stone fireplace on one wall. It would make an ideal place to meet after a long day on the slopes, too!

HAMMEL STUDIO

The Hammel office studio has a sleek modern style everyone today loves. With a covered patio, a full bath with a walk-in shower, a kitchenette, and a spot for a stackable washer and dryer, this structure can easily convert to a stylish studio apartment or provide multiple functions with no problem.

PLAN #C19-011D-0603

312 square feet of living area
width: 26'   depth: 12'
1 bedroom, 1 bath
building height: 10'-6"
2" x 6" exterior walls
slab foundation

OFFICE / STUDIO
16'/6" X 11/4"
(8' CLG)

FOLD'G WALL HUNG TABLE

W
D

OPEN SHLVS

© copyright by designer/architect

efficient kitchen

PATIO

large covered patio

Blueprint PRICING and ORDERING + VISIT houseplansandmore.com + 1-800-373-2646

ELLENDALE PAVILION

PLAN #C19-009D-7530

814 square feet of living area
width: 24'   depth: 47'
1 bath
building height: 15'-6"
slab foundation

A vaulted ceiling with skylights, a hot tub, a kitchen/bar, a sauna room, and a full bath highlight this design. Located at the rear is a 24' x 12' covered vaulted patio with outdoor fireplace and optional skylights. Add an outdoor grill and you have an exceptional party space or poolside structure.

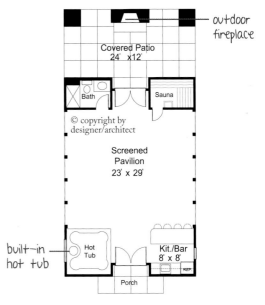

outdoor fireplace

Covered Patio
24' x12'

Bath

Sauna

© copyright by designer/architect

Screened Pavilion
23' x 29'

built-in hot tub

Hot Tub

Kit./Bar
8' x 8'

Porch

SUMMERVILLE
A bath and an open bar featuring a designated wall for a TV are conveniently located on the porch and patio of this adorable poolside cabana. Take a seat, grab a drink, and enjoy life!

PLAN #C19-009D-7524
112 square feet of living area
width: 22'   depth: 24'
1 bath
building height: 16'-6"
slab foundation

WESLAN
For those of you who can't tear away from your favorite hobbies and home projects, this workshop includes a full bath and plenty of space for those late nights when you decide to crash on the couch.

PLAN #C19-142D-4503
450 square feet of living area
width: 15'   depth: 30'
1 bath
building height: 13'-6"
slab foundation

AURORA PEAK
An outdoor lodge getaway has a vaulted interior with rustic beams and a cozy fireplace. There's a large outdoor deck, perfect for grilling, dining, or sunning. A perfect après skiing spot to relax.

PLAN #C19-142D-7506
306 square feet of living area
width: 22'-6"   depth: 21'
building height: 16'-5"
slab foundation

CABANA COVE
Take entertaining to a whole new level with this poolside structure, featuring an activity room, an island kitchen, a bedroom, bath, and covered porch with a cozy outdoor fireplace.

PLAN #C19-055D-1029
1117 square feet of living area
width: 62'   depth: 50'-6"
1 bedroom, 1 bath
building height: 24'
crawl space or slab foundation,
please specify when ordering

AVA LAGO
The perfect poolside structure to entice all family members to come outside and stay awhile. This vaulted cabana has a large wet bar and lanai space, including a half bath, a barn door-style TV cabinet, and a huge storage area for yard equipment and pool supplies.

PLAN #C19-142D-7555
586 square feet of living area
width: 26' depth: 24'
$^1/_2$ bath
building height: 16'-9"
slab foundation

RITA
This modern-style cabana features an outdoor kitchen with plenty of outdoor dining space, a spacious open living area inside, a room perfect as a bedroom, and a full bath.

PLAN #C19-113D-7509
360 square feet of living area
width: 28' depth: 28'
1 bedroom, 1 bath
monolithic slab foundation standard;
crawl space or floating slab available for a fee

LARONDA
The first floor has a game room sports bar including a fireplace, a kitchen/wet bar, a bath, and a movie theater with a 10' wide screen, The lower level has a rear entry garage, shop area, and storage room

PLAN #C19-009D-7533
960 square feet of living area
width: 34' depth: 32'
1 bath
building height: 17'
walk-out basement foundation

LONG
A modern studio that looks perfect with the ever-popular modern farmhouse architecture style. Plenty of storage and a full bath with an oversized shower make this a very versatile choice as in-law quarters, too.

PLAN #C19-165D-7500
480 square feet of living area
width: 30' depth: 16'
1 bath
building height: 13'-2"
2" x 6" exterior walls
slab foundation

STACY
This structure quite possibly could be the cutest rental property or mother-in-law cottage ever! With a vaulted living room, a kitchen with stackable washer/dryer space, a bedroom with a walk-in closet, and a full bath, it truly has it all.

PLAN #C19-130D-0362
395 square feet of living area
width: 16'   depth: 24'-8"
1 bedroom, 1 bath
building height: 14'
slab foundation standard;
crawl space or basement available for a fee

DESTINY
This music studio can also easily be used as a guest house. Inside you'll find a vaulted control room with kitchenette, a separate foyer for privacy, a half bath, and a vaulted sound room that could be a comfortable bedroom.

PLAN #C19-142D-7522
413 square feet of living area
width: 22'   depth: 18'-9"
$1/2$ bath
building height: 13'-6"
slab foundation

MOORPARK
A timeless gabled structure featuring a vaulted living area that can also be used for sleeping space. Space-saving table design, a wardrobe closet, a kitchenette, and full bath complete the layout.

PLAN #C19-012D-7507
322 square feet of living area
width: 14'   depth: 23'
1 bedroom, 1 bath
joisted crawl space or post & beam foundation standard; slab or basement available for a fee

ELLEN
The ideal shelter for a hot tub or screened dining, including a vaulted ceiling, a cozy outdoor fireplace, a convenient kitchen, and a bathroom. Rear storage is also included.

PLAN #C19-009D-7528
374 square feet of living area
width: 17'   depth: 22'
1 bath
building height: 17'
slab foundation

MORETTO BEND
This small cottage makes a charming home office space or guest house. With multiple built-ins making storage abundant, it would be easy to remain ultra organized and neat in such a small space.

PLAN #C19-063D-7500
144 square feet of living area
width: 12' depth: 16'
2" x 6" exterior walls
building height: 14'-6"
slab foundation

BANFF
A studio/home office completely flooded with sunlight from large windows all around and above. Double French doors access a covered porch, creating a lovely outdoor area. There's also a loft area above the bath for storage.

PLAN #C19-063D-7501
432 square feet of living area
width: 20' depth: 30'
building height: 20'
$\frac{1}{2}$ bath
2" x 6" exterior walls
slab foundation

MARTINA
This is the perfect vaulted studio, making it an ideal artist's retreat or craft workshop. Double French doors easily access the covered porch, adding plenty of additional sunlight, too.

PLAN #C19-063D-7505
288 square feet of living area
width: 20' depth: 16'
building height: 16'-8"
2" x 6" exterior walls
crawl space or slab foundation, please specify when ordering

MILES
This rustic cabana features an outdoor kitchen with grill, a range, refrigerator, and a sink for easy outdoor entertaining. The interior has an open space with a kitchenette, a large bath, and a bedroom.

PLAN #C19-113D-7508
360 square feet of living area
width: 28' depth: 20'
1 bedroom, 1 bath
monolithic slab standard;
crawl space or floating slab available for a fee

MORROW
The vaulted interior creates openness that's appreciated in this small footprint. The living area doubles as sleeping space, or make this an ideal in-law suite. There's a fold-down space-saving table for mealtime, a kitchenette, and a bath with a walk-in shower.

PLAN #C19-012D-7508
322 square feet of living area
width: 14'   depth: 23'
1 bath
joisted crawl space or post & beam foundation standard; slab or basement available for a fee

KELLIANNE
This could be the perfect office, thanks to an entry closet, an extra storage closet, a toilet room, and a staircase to a basement storm shelter providing additional function.

PLAN #C19-009D-7507
350 square feet of living area
width: 24'   depth: 36'
1 bedroom, 1/2 bath
building height: 18'
basement foundation

Blueprint PRICING and ORDERING + VISIT houseplansandmore.com + 1-800-373-2646

CHANDLER LANE
This clever structure is part garage, but it also creates an ideal spot for an outdoor kitchen and grill under a covered side porch. It can also shield garbage receptacles from the weather.

PLAN #C19-032D-1005
384 square feet of living area
width: 16'   depth: 24'
building height: 13'-8"
2" x 6" exterior walls
floating slab or monolithic slab foundation, please specify when ordering

CAREFREE
This studio pool house is open and perfect for stepping out of the sun and cooling off. It could also be used as guest or in-law quarters since it has a full bath and a large storage closet.

PLAN #C19-142D-7520
385 square feet of living area
width: 18'   depth: 24'
1 bath
building height: 14'-6"
concrete block exterior walls
slab foundation

TINLEY
A great design for weekend fun! This would be ideal as a fishing/hunting camp. There's an insulated bunk room and a vaulted screened porch that keeps insects out while still allowing a breeze to flow through. Find plenty of storage under the bunk room.

PLAN #C19-124D-7500
192 square feet of living area
width: 12'   depth: 16'
1 bedroom
building height: 11'-4"
crawl space foundation

MIRAGE
This modern cabana cottage would be amazing as guest quarters or when entertaining poolside. It includes an open island kitchen, a fireplace, space for a stackable washer/dryer, two bedrooms, a bath, and a covered porch ideal for an outdoor kitchen.

PLAN #C19-126D-1153
776 square feet of living area
width: 40'   depth: 26'
2 bedrooms, 1 bath
building height: 21'
2" x 6" exterior walls
slab foundation

SUMMERSUN
This fun pool pavilion has a walk-up bar, a sauna room, and a full bath with two storage rooms to the rear. Create memories all summer around your pool or patio with this fun place!

PLAN #C19-009D-7527
151 square feet of living area
width: 26'   depth: 17'
1 bath
building height: 13'
slab foundation

VINCE
This is a the perfect place to relax while the kids play, and the multiple windows allow for great views from every side so you can always keep your eye on them when they head outdoors.

PLAN #C19-124D-7501
192 square feet of living area
width: 12'   depth: 16'
building height: 11'-4"
crawl space foundation

SHEDS

Whether you're a gardening enthusiast looking for some additional space or the family handyman longing for a workshop or hobby storage area, this selection of sheds will be ideal for so many different needs. Browse through this selection and then order online, or find countless more shed plans at houseplansandmore.com.

KORBIN
The classic look of this barn-style shed is a great country-style accessory for your yard. The covered side porch offers dry storage for firewood and other items, guarding them from the elements.

PLAN #C19-160D-4500
168 square feet
width: 19' depth: 14'
building height: 16'
raised wood floor or slab foundation,
please specify when ordering

MAXINE
This attractive shed has clerestory windows for added light. With an interior rear wall height of 7'-3" and a 5' x 6'-9" double-door, this shed is easy to access.

PLAN #C19-002D-4515
includes 3 sizes:
10' x 10'   12' x 10'   14' x 10'
building height: 10'-11"
wood floor on 4x6 runners foundation
material list/instructions included

MONACA
The perfect option for garden storage that offers a convenient double-entry door for storing gardening supplies and tools easily.

PLAN #C19-002D-4519
80 square feet
width: 10' depth: 8'
building height: 9'-6"
wood floor on 4x4 runners foundation
material list/instructions included

DOMANI
This sleek modern-style shed makes additional storage far from an eyesore. Built-in windows add daylight, making it easy to locate its contents, and the style is a great backyard focal point.

PLAN #C19-127D-4514
9 sizes available:
12'x8'   12'x10'   12'x12'
14'x8'   14'x10'   14'x12'
16'x8'   16'x10'   16'x12'
wood floor on concrete block foundation
construction prints are $8^{1}/_{2}$" x 11"

MONESSEN
This shed offers complete flexibility since it can be built to be as big as 16' x 8' or as small as 8' x 8', whatever works best for your needs and your lot size. Total flexibility is a great feature!

PLAN #C19-002D-4500
3 sizes included
8' x 8'   12' x 8'   16' x 8'
building height: 8'-2"
wood floor on gravel base or slab foundation, please specify when ordering
material list/instructions included

MARCELLA
The 8' x 7' overhead garage-style door makes entry with large equipment easy. Several windows add light to the interior, offering ease when trying to locate items inside.

PLAN #C19-002D-4521
192 square feet
width: 12'   depth: 16'
building height: 12'-5"
slab foundation
material list/instructions included

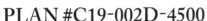

Blueprint PRICING and ORDERING + VISIT houseplansandmore.com + 1-800-373-2646

MERRILL
Attractive window boxes, operable windows, and a 2' deep front covered porch make this shed playhouse so charming! With a ceiling height of 6'-1", the kids will love it in warmer months.

PLAN #C19-002D-4505
64 square feet
width: 8'   depth: 8'
building height: 9'-2"
wood floor on 4x4 runners foundation
material list/instructions included

MARIANNA
This taller-style shed enjoys a barnyard look thanks to its Gambrel roof style. This shed would look great near your garden or anywhere on your property, especially in a rural setting.

PLAN #C19-002D-4501
includes 3 sizes
12' x 12'   12' x 16'   12' x 20'
building height: 12'-10"
wood floor on concrete pier or slab foundation, please specify when ordering
material list/instructions included

SELLERSVILLE
This shed partners with adolescent fun time by offering a storage solution that can also be used as a children's playhouse, featuring a cute outdoor balcony.

PLAN #C19-002D-4514
144 square feet
width: 12'   depth: 12'
building height: 14'-1"
wood floor on concrete pier or slab foundation, please specify when ordering
material list/instructions included

MADDY
The perfect all-purpose shed design features a garage door style entry as well as another side entry door. Two windows brighten the interior superbly.

PLAN #C19-002D-4506
192 square feet
width: 16'   depth: 12'
building height: 12'-5"
slab foundation
material list/instructions included

Blueprint PRICING and ORDERING + VISIT houseplansandmore.com + 1-800-373-2646

RASMUSSEN
This charming barn-style shed matches true country style without a hitch. Double front doors and a Gambrel-style roof create an easy-to-use interior space.

PLAN #C19-002D-4520
120 square feet
width: 10'   depth: 12'
building height: 10'-7"
wood floor on 4x4 runners foundation
material list/instructions included

BOSCOBEL
Absolutely the perfect garden shed with plenty of light in the interior, providing an ideal place for seedlings to flourish in colder temperatures.

PLAN #C19-002D-4523
100 square feet
width: 10'   depth: 10'
building height: 11'-4"
wood floor on 4x4 runners foundation
material list/instructions included

BLONDELL
This classic shed style looks great in any backyard setting. Use it to store yard equipment, patio furniture in the off-season, or gardening supplies.

PLAN #C19-002D-4504
includes 3 sizes:
10' x 12'   10' x 16'   10' x 20'
building height: 8'-9"
wood floor on 4x4 runners foundation
material list/instructions included

MAUDE
This garden shed has large skylight windows for optimal plant growth and ample room for tool and lawn equipment storage, too. Start enjoying your own organic veggies year-round with help from this handy shed!

PLAN #C19-002D-4507
120 square feet
width: 10'   depth: 12'
building height: 9'-9"
wood floor on gravel base foundation
material list/instructions included

CARMEN COVE
Available in three popular sizes, these mini barns provide an ample storage solution for your lawn or garden equipment and includes a 4' x 6'-4" double-door for easy access.

PLAN #C19-002D-4502
includes 3 sizes:
10' x 12'   10' x 16'   10' x 20'
building height: 8'-5"
wood floor on 4x4 runners foundation
material list/instructions included

HERNDON
This shed would make the best and most comfortable workshop. With its covered front porch and three windows, it would be the perfect spot for the family handyman to work without distractions!

PLAN #C19-002D-7520
width: 24'   depth: 20'
building height: 13'-6"
slab foundation
material list/instructions included

NOVAK
This economical and easy-to-build modern-inspired shed features a barn-style sliding door entry with a transom above for added light to the interior. The stylish solution for your storage needs!

PLAN #C19-165D-4502
192 square feet
width: 16'   depth: 12'
building height: 12'-6"
2" x 6" exterior walls
slab foundation

MARCIA
The Gambrel roof design on this storage shed gives it a pleasing country style. It allows easy access thanks to its 5'-6" x 6'-8" double-door entry.

PLAN #C19-002D-4508
includes 3 sizes:
12' x 8'   12' x 12'   12' x 16'
building height: 9'-10"
wood floor on concrete pier or slab foundation, please specify when ordering
material list/instructions included

Blueprint PRICING and ORDERING + VISIT houseplansandmore.com + 1-800-373-2646

MARILYN
This cheerful shed with porch and firewood storage has a friendly double window brightening the interior. Designed to appear like a cottage, it has a convenient overhang, perfect for storing firewood.

PLAN #C19-125D-4501
122 square feet
width: 17'   depth: 12'
building height: 16'-10"
slab foundation

BOXWOOD
An attractive shed, ideal for providing stylish storage right in your backyard. Popular barn-style sliding doors make yard equipment and gardening supplies super easy to access.

PLAN #C19-165D-4501
160 square feet
width: 16'   depth: 10'
building height: 12'-3"
2" x 6" exterior walls
slab foundation

BLAINE
With a perfect 3' x 6'-8" Dutch-style door, this shed is ideal for storage or as a fun playhouse for children. Shutters and a window box create a charming exterior that will look great in any backyard.

PLAN #C19-002D-4522
72 square feet
width: 12' depth: 8'
building height: 10'-5"
wood floor on 4x4 runners foundation
material list/instructions included

SHAW
This sleek shed would look fantastic with any style of home, but especially with the modern farmhouse style. It would be the perfect spot for potting plants since it includes Double French doors and a window illuminating the interior perfectly for any task at hand.

PLAN #C19-165D-4500
420 square feet
width: 30' depth: 14'
building height: 12'-8"
2" x 6" exterior walls
slab foundation

PENNEY
The perfect rustic Craftsman shed offers a double-door entry into the inside for ease and also a covered front porch, making it a nice place to relax or store firewood in a dry, sheltered place.

PLAN #C19-142D-4501
150 square feet of living area
width: 15' depth: 15'
building height: 14'
wood floor joists over treated girders foundation

JENNAR
With wide double-doors that open to the inside and its wraparound covered porch design, this shed is perfect for firewood storage. The decorative dormer adds light to the interior and great style to the exterior.

PLAN #C19-125D-4502
151 square feet of living area
width: 19' depth: 17'
building height: 16'
slab foundation

NORRIS
An attractive-style shed that is perfect for storage of lawn and garden equipment, this shed also includes a 4' x 6' double-door for easy access.

PLAN #C19-002D-4524
   includes 4 sizes:
   8' x 8' 8' x 10' 8' x 12' 8' x 16"
   building height: 7'-6"
   wood floor on 4x4 runners foundation
   material list/instructions included

JOANIE
This is the perfect option for a garden workshop or "she" shed if the kids don't want to make it into their own adorable playhouse! A covered front porch and double window boxes take its charm to a new level.

PLAN #C19-142D-4500
   192 square feet
   width: 16' depth: 16'
   building height: 11'-4"
   slab foundation

TOLAND PLACE
The perfect open floor plan, providing ample workspace and additional storage with a handy loft above. A side garage door makes entry easy.

PLAN #C19-005D-7500
   1150 square feet
   width: 30' depth: 22'
   building height: 20'-6"
   slab foundation
   material list included

GAVIER
The perfect little Victorian-inspired shed has both a single door with access to the loft and a double door into the storage area.

PLAN #C19-127D-4510
   322 square feet
   width: 14' depth: 13'
   building height: 15'-7"
   wood floor on concrete blocks foundation
   construction prints are 8½" x 11"

HOW CAN I FIND OUT IF I CAN AFFORD TO BUILD?

GET AN ACCURATE ESTIMATED COST-TO-BUILD REPORT

The most important question for someone wanting to build a new home is, "How much is it going to cost?" Obviously, you must have an accurate budget set prior to ordering house plans and beginning construction, or your dream home will quickly turn into a nightmare. Our goal is to make building your home a much simpler reality that's within reach, thanks to the estimated cost-to-build report available for all of the plans in this book and on our website, houseplansandmore.com.

Price is always the number-one factor when selecting a new home. Price dictates the size and the quality of materials you will choose. So, it comes as no surprise that having an accurate building estimate prior to making your final decision on a home plan is quite possibly the most important step in the entire process.

If you feel you've found "the" home, then before taking the step of purchasing plans, order an estimated cost-to-build report for the zip code where you want to build. When you order this report created specifically for you, it will educate you on all costs associated with building your new home. Simply order the cost-to-build report on houseplansandmore.com for the home you want to build and gain knowledge of the material and labor cost associated with the home. Not only does the report allow you to choose the quality of the materials, you can also select options in every aspect of the project, from lot condition to contractor fees. This report will allow you to successfully manage your construction budget in all areas, clearly see where the majority of the costs lie, and save you money from start to finish.

Listed below are the categories included in every cost-to-build report. Each category breaks down labor cost, material cost, and funds needed, and the report offers the ability to manipulate over/under-adjustments if necessary.

BASIC INFORMATION includes your contact information, the state and zip code where you intend to build. First, select material class. It will include details of the home such as square footage, number of windows, fireplaces, balconies, and bathrooms. Deck, basement, or bonus room square footage is included. Lot size and garage location and number of bays are also included.

GENERAL SOFT COSTS include cost for plans, customizing (if applicable), building permits, pre-construction services, and planning expenses.

SITE WORK & UTILITIES include water, sewer, electric, and gas. Choose the type of site work you will need prior to building and if you'll need a driveway.

FOUNDATION is selected from a menu that lists the most common types.

FRAMING ROUGH SHELL calculates your rough framing costs, including framing for fireplaces, balconies, decks, porches, basements, and bonus rooms.

ROOFING includes several options so you can see how it will affect your overall price.

DRY OUT SHELL allows you to select doors, windows, siding and garage doors.

ELECTRICAL includes wiring and the quality of the light fixtures.

PLUMBING includes plumbing materials, plumbing fixtures, and fireproofing materials. It includes labor costs and the ability to change fixture quality.

HVAC includes costs for both labor and materials.

INSULATION includes costs for both labor and materials.

FINISH SHELL includes drywall, interior doors and trim, stairs, shower doors, mirrors, and bath accessories - costs for both labor and materials.

CABINETS & VANITIES select the grade of your cabinets, vanities, kitchen countertops, and bathroom vanity materials, as well as appliances.

PAINTING includes all painting materials, their quality, and labor.

FLOORING includes over a dozen flooring material options.

SPECIAL EQUIPMENT NEEDS calculate cost for unforeseen expenses.

CONTRACTOR FEE / PROJECT MANAGER includes the cost of your cost-to-build report, project manager, and/or general contractor fees. If you're doing the managing yourself, your costs will be tremendously lower in this portion.

LAND PAYOFF includes the cost of your land.

RESERVES/CLOSING COSTS includes interest, contingency reserves, and closing costs.

We've taken the guesswork out of what your new home will cost. Take control of your homebuilding project, determine the major expenses upfront, and save money. Easily supervise all costs, from labor to materials. Manage your home building with confidence and avoid costly mistakes and unforeseen expenses. If you want to order a cost-to-build report for a home plan, visit houseplansandmore.com and search for the plan. Then, look for the orange button that says "Request Your Report" and get started.

OUR BLUEPRINT PACKAGES INCLUDE

FIND OUT WHAT IS TYPICALLY INCLUDED

A quality home – one that looks good, functions well, and provides years of enjoyment – is a product of many things: design, materials, and craftsmanship. But it's also the result of outstanding blueprints – the actual plans and specifications that tell the builder exactly how to build your home.

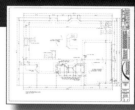

And with our **BLUEPRINT PACKAGES** you get the absolute best. A complete set of blueprints is available for every design in this book. These "working drawings" are highly detailed, resulting in two key benefits:

- **BETTER UNDERSTANDING BY THE CONTRACTOR OF HOW TO BUILD YOUR HOME AND...**

- **MORE ACCURATE CONSTRUCTION ESTIMATES THAT WILL SAVE YOU TIME AND MONEY.**

Below is a description of the plan information included for most of the designs in this book. Specific details may vary with each designer's plan. While this information is typical for most plans, we cannot assure the inclusion of all the following referenced items.

Please contact us at 1-800-373-2646 for a specific plan's information.

COVER SHEET is the artist's rendering of the home's exterior. It gives you an idea of how the home will look when finished.

FOUNDATION plan shows the layout of the specific foundation type you've chosen with all notations and dimensions included. See the specific plan page for the foundation types available. If a home plan doesn't have your desired foundation type, please call 1-800-373-2646 and we'll advise you on how to customize the plan to include the foundation you need.

FLOOR PLANS show wall placement, doors, closets, plumbing fixtures, electrical outlets, columns, and beams.

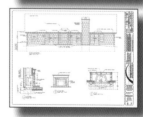

INTERIOR ELEVATIONS provide views of interior elements such as fireplaces, kitchen cabinets, built-in units, and other features of the home.

EXTERIOR ELEVATIONS illustrate the front, rear, and sides of the house and include the required dimensions and exterior material details.

SECTIONS show detailed views of the home or portions of the home as if it were sliced from the roof to the foundation. This shows load-bearing walls, stairs, joists, trusses, and other structural elements.

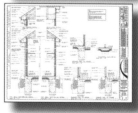

DETAILS show how to construct certain components such as the roof system, stairs, deck, etc.

WHAT KIND OF PLAN PACKAGE DO YOU NEED?

SELECT THE TYPE OF BLUEPRINT THAT BEST FITS YOUR SITUATION

Please note: Not all plan packages are available for every plan. To see all of the plan options currently available, please visit houseplansandmore.com or call 1-800-373-2646.

5-SET PLAN PACKAGE includes five complete sets of construction drawings. Besides one set for yourself, additional sets of blueprints will be required for your lender, your local building department, your contractor, and any other tradespeople working on your project. Please note: These 5 sets of plans are copyrighted, so they can't be altered or copied.

8-SET PLAN PACKAGE includes eight complete sets of construction drawings. Besides one set for yourself, additional sets of blueprints will be required for your lender, your local building department, your contractor, and any other tradespeople working on your project. Please note: These 8 sets of plans are copyrighted, so they can't be altered or copied.

REPRODUCIBLE MASTERS is one complete paper set of construction drawings that can be modified. They include a one-time build copyright release that allows you to draw changes on the plans. This allows you, your builder, or local design professional to make the necessary drawing changes without the major expense of entirely redrawing the plans. Easily make minor drawing changes by using correction fluid to cover up small areas of the existing drawing, then draw in your modifications. Once the plan has been altered to fit your needs, you have the right to copy or reproduce the modified plans as needed for building your home.

Please note: The right of building only one home from these plans is licensed exclusively to the buyer. You may not use this design to build a second or multiple dwelling(s) without purchasing a multi-build license.

PDF FILE FORMAT is our most popular plan option because of how fast you can receive them (usually within 24 to 48 hours Monday through Friday), and their ability to be easily shared via email with your contractor, subcontractors, and local building officials. The PDF file format is a complete set of construction drawings in an electronic file format. It includes a one-time build copyright release that allows you to make changes and copies of the plans. Typically you will receive a PDF file via email within 24-48 hours (Mon-Fri, 7:30am-4:30pm CST), allowing you to save money on shipping. Upon receiving, visit a local copy or print shop and print the number of plans you need to build your home, or print one and alter the plan by using correction fluid and drawing in your modifications.

Please note: These are flat image files and cannot be altered electronically. PDF files are nonrefundable and not returnable.

CAD FILE FORMAT is the actual computer files for a plan directly from AutoCAD or another computer-aided design program. CAD files are the best option if you have a significant amount of changes to make to the plan or if you need to make the plan fit your local codes. If you purchase a CAD file, it allows you or a local design professional the ability to modify the plans electronically in a CAD program, so making changes to the plan is easier and less expensive than using a paper set of plans when modifying. A CAD package also includes a one-time build copyright release that allows you to legally make your changes, and print multiple copies of the plan. See the specific plan page for availability and pricing.

Please note: CAD files are nonrefundable and not returnable.

MIRROR REVERSE SETS Sometimes a home fits a site better if it is flipped left to right. A mirror reverse set of plans is simply a mirror image of the original drawings, causing the lettering and dimensions to read backwards. Therefore, when ordering a mirror reverse set of plans, you must purchase at least one set of the original plans to read from, and use the mirror reverse set for construction. Some plans offer right-reading reverse for an additional fee. This means the plan has been redrawn by the designer as the mirrored version and can easily be read.

ADDITIONAL SETS You can order additional sets of a plan for an additional fee. A 5-set, 8-set, or reproducible master must have been previously purchased.

Please note: Only available within 90 days after purchase of a plan package.

2" X 6" EXTERIOR WALLS 2" x 6" exterior walls can be purchased for some plans for an additional fee (see the specific plan at houseplansandmore.com for availability and pricing).

DO YOU WANT TO MAKE CHANGES TO YOUR PLAN?

We understand that sometimes it is difficult to find blueprints that meet all of your specific needs.
That is why we offer home plan modification services so you can build a home exactly the way you want it!

ARE YOU THINKING ABOUT CUSTOMIZING A PLAN?

If you're like many customers, you want to make changes to the home plan you've chosen to make it the dream home you've always wanted. That's where our expert design and modification partners come in. You won't find a more efficient and economic way to get your changes done than by using our customizing services.

Whether it's enlarging a kitchen, adding a porch, or converting a crawl space to a basement, we can customize any plan and make it perfect for you. Simply create your wish list and let us go to work. Soon you'll have the customized blueprints for your new home, and at a fraction of the cost of hiring a local architect!

IT'S EASY!

- We can customize any plan in this book.
- We provide a FREE cost estimate for your home plan modifications within 24-48 hours (Monday-Friday, 7:30am-4:30pm CST).
- Average turn-around time to complete the modifications is typically 2-3 weeks.
- You will receive one-on-one design consultations.

CUSTOMIZING FACTS

- The average cost to have a house plan customized is typically less than 1% of the building costs - compare that to the national average of 7% of building costs.
- The average modification cost for a home is typically $800 to $1,500. This does not include the cost of purchasing the PDF file format of the blueprints, which is required to legally make the plan modifications.

OTHER HELPFUL INFO

- Sketch or make a specific list of changes you'd like to make on the Home Plan Modification Request Form.
- A home plan modification specialist will contact you within 1-2 business days with your free estimate.
- Upon accepting the estimate, you will need to purchase the PDF or CAD file format.
- A contract, which includes a specific list of changes and fees, will be sent to you prior for your approval.
- Upon approval, your modification specialist will keep you informed by emailing sketches of the project.
- Plans can be converted to metric, or to a Barrier-free layout (also referred to as a universal home design, which allows easier mobility for an individual with limitations of any kind).

2 EASY STEPS

1 VISIT houseplansandmore.com and click on the Resources tab at the top of the home page, or scan the QR code to the right to download the Home Plan Modification Request Form.

2 EMAIL your completed form to: customizehpm@designamerica.com.
   If you're unable to access the Internet, please call us at 1-800-373-2646
   (Monday-Friday, 7:30am - 4:30pm CST).

OTHER HELPFUL BUILDING AIDS

Your blueprints will contain all of the necessary construction information you need to build your home. But, we also offer the following products and services to save you time and money in the building process.

MATERIAL LIST Many of the home plans in this book have a material list available for purchase that gives you the quantity, dimensions, and description of the building materials needed to construct the home (see the specific plan at houseplansandmore.com for availability and pricing). Keep in mind, due to variations in local building code requirements, exact material quantities cannot be guaranteed.

Please note: Material lists are created with the standard foundation type only. Please review the material list and the construction drawings with your material supplier to verify measurements and quantities of the material listed before ordering supplies.

THE LEGAL KIT Avoid many legal pitfalls and build your home with confidence using the forms and contracts featured in this kit. Included are request for proposal documents, various fixed price and cost plus contracts, instructions on how and when to use each form, warranty statements, and more. Save time and money before you break ground on your new home or start a remodeling project. All forms are reproducible. This kit is ideal for homebuilders and contractors.

Cost: $35.00

DETAIL PLAN PACKAGES - ELECTRICAL, FRAMING & PLUMBING Three separate packages offer homebuilders details for constructing various foundations; numerous floor, wall, and roof framing techniques; simple to complex residential wiring; sump and water softener hookups; plumbing connection methods; installation of septic systems; and more. Each package includes three-dimensional illustrations and a glossary of terms.

Purchase one or all three. Cost: $20.00 each, or all three for $40.00. Please note: These drawings do not pertain to a specific home plan, but they include general guidelines and tips for construction in all three of these trades.

EXPRESS DELIVERY Most orders are processed within 24 hours of receipt. Please allow 7-10 business days for standard delivery. If you need to place a rush order, please call us by 11:00 am Monday-Friday CST and ask for express service (allow 1-2 business days).

Please see page 238 for specific pricing information for shipping and handling.

TECHNICAL ASSISTANCE If you have questions about your blueprints, we offer technical assistance by calling 1-314-770-2228 (Monday-Friday, 7:30am-4:30pm CST). Whether it involves design modifications or field assistance, our home plans team is extremely familiar with all of our designs and will be happy to help you. We want your home to be everything you expect it to be.

BEFORE YOU ORDER

Please note: Plan pricing is subject to change without notice.
For current pricing, visit houseplansandmore.com or call us at 1-800-373-2646.

BUILDING CODE REQUIREMENTS At the time the construction drawings were prepared, every effort was made to ensure that these plans and specifications met nationally recognized codes. These plans conform to most national building codes. Because building codes vary from area to area, some drawing modifications and/or the assistance of a professional designer or architect may be necessary to comply with your local codes or to accommodate your specific building site conditions. We advise you to consult with your local building official or a local builder for information regarding codes governing your area prior to ordering blueprints.

COPYRIGHT Plans are protected under Copyright Law. Reproduction by any means is strictly prohibited. The right of building only one structure from all plan packages is licensed exclusively to the buyer, and the plans may not be resold unless by express written authorization from the home designer or architect. You may not use this design to build a second or multiple structure(s) without purchasing a multi-build license. Each violation of the copyright law is punishable by a fine.

LICENSE TO BUILD When you purchase a "full set of construction drawings" from Design America, Inc., you are purchasing an exclusive one-time "License to Build," not the rights to the design. Design America, Inc.," is granting you permission on behalf of the plan's designer or architect to use the construction drawings one time for the building of the home. The construction drawings (also referred to as blueprints/plans and any derivative of that plan, whether extensive or minor) are still owned and protected under copyright laws by the original designer. The blueprints/plans cannot be resold, transferred, rented, loaned, or used by anyone other than the original purchaser of the "License to Build" without written consent from Design America, Inc., or the plan designer. If you are interested in building the plan more than once, please call 1-800-373-2646 and inquire about purchasing a Multi-Build License that will allow you to build a home design more than one time.

Please note: A "full set of construction drawings" consists of either CAD files or PDF files.

EXCHANGE POLICY Since blueprints are printed in response to your order, we cannot honor requests for refunds.

SHIPPING & HANDLING CHARGES

U.S. SHIPPING
(AK and HI express only)

Regular (allow 7-10 business days)	$30.00
Priority (allow 3-5 business days)	$50.00
Express* (allow 1-2 business days)	$70.00

CANADA SHIPPING**

Regular (allow 8-12 business days)	$50.00
Express* (allow 3-5 business days)	$100.00

OVERSEAS SHIPPING/INTERNATIONAL
For shipping costs, please call or email (customerservice@designamerica.com)

* For express delivery please call us by 11:00 am Monday-Friday CST

** Orders may be subject to custom's fees and or duties/taxes.

Note: Shipping & handling does not apply on PDF and CAD File orders. PDF and CAD orders will be emailed within 24-48 hours (Monday - Friday, 7:30 am - 4:30 pm CST) of purchase.

ORDER FORM

PLEASE NOTE: Plan pricing is subject to change without notice. For current pricing, visit houseplansandmore.com or call us at 1-800-373-2646.

Please send me the following:

Plan Number: C19-_____

Select Foundation Type:

(Select ONE- see plan page for available options).

☐ Slab   ☐ Crawl space   ☐ Basement

☐ Walk-out basement   ☐ Pier   ☐ Other

☐ Optional foundation for an additional fee

    Enter additional foundation cost $_____

      (see houseplansandmore.com for pricing)

PLAN PACKAGE   COST

☐ CAD File $_____

☐ PDF File Format (recommended) $_____

☐ Reproducible Masters $_____

☐ 8-Set Plan Package $_____

☐ 5-Set Plan Package $_____

Visit houseplansandmore.com to see current pricing and all plan package options available.

IMPORTANT EXTRAS

For pricing and availability of Material Lists and other plan options listed below, visit houseplansandmore.com or call 1-800-373-2646.

☐ Additional plan sets*:

    _____ set(s) at $_____ per set $_____

☐ Print in mirror reverse:

    _____ set(s) at $_____ per set $_____

    (where right-reading reverse is not available)

☐ Print in right-reading reverse:

    one-time additional fee of $_____ $_____

☐ Material List $_____

☐ Legal Kit (001D-9991, see page 237) $_____

Detail Plan Packages: (see page 237)

    ☐ Framing   ☐ Electrical   ☐ Plumbing $_____

    (001D-9992)   (001D-9993)   (001D-9994)

Shipping (see page 238) $_____

SUBTOTAL $_____

Sales Tax (MO residents only, add 8.425%) $_____

TOTAL $_____

*Available only within 90 days after purchase of plan

HELPFUL TIPS

■ You can upgrade to a different plan package within 90 days of your original plan purchase.

■ Additional sets cannot be ordered without the purchase of a 5-Set, 8-Set, or Reproducible Masters.

Name _____

      (Please print or type)

Street _____

      (Please do not use a P.O. Box)

City _____

State _____

Country _____ Zip _____

Daytime telephone __(_____)_____

E-Mail _____

      (For invoice and tracking info)

Payment   ☐ Bank check/money order.
      No personal checks.

Make check/money order payable to Design America, Inc.

☐ MasterCard   ☐ VISA   ☐ DISCOVER   ☐ AMERICAN EXPRESS Cards

Credit card number _____

Expiration date (mm/yy)_____

CID _____

Signature_____

☐ I hereby authorize Design America, Inc., to charge this purchase to my credit card.

Please check the appropriate box:

☐ Building home for myself

☐ I'm building the home for someone else

ORDER ONLINE houseplansandmore.com

ORDER TOLL-FREE BY PHONE

1-800-373-2646   Fax: 314-770-2226

EXPRESS DELIVERY

Most orders are processed within 24 hours of receipt. If you need to place a rush order, please call us by 11:00 am CST and ask for express service.

Business Hours: Monday-Friday (7:30am-4:30pm CST)

MAIL YOUR ORDER

Design America, Inc.
734 West Port Plaza, Suite #208
St. Louis, MO 63146

SOURCE CODE C19

INDEX

PHOTO CREDITS

Unless noted below, all photos and images throughout this publication have been provided by the designer/architect: page 2 - photo featuring home by REAL LOG HOMES®, realloghomes.com, photographer Roger Wade Studios; page 3 - photo courtesy of REAL LOG HOMES®, realloghomes.com, photographer James Ray Spahn; page 4 - photo courtesy of REAL LOG HOMES®, realloghomes.com, photographer James Ray Spahn; page 6 - photo bottom, left courtesy of REAL LOG HOMES®, realloghomes.com, photographer Rich Frutchey; page 7 - REAL LOG HOMES®, realloghomes.com, photographer James Ray Spahn; page 9 - photo courtesy of REAL LOG HOMES®, realloghomes.com, photographer Roger Wade Studios; page 48 - photo courtesy of ClosetMaid®; page 103 - Photo courtesy of R-Control® SIPs; page 123 - photo bottom, right courtesy of REAL LOG HOMES®, realloghomes.com, photographer James Ray Spahn; page 178 - photo top, right courtesy of ClosetMaid®; photo bottom, right courtesy of istockphoto; page 179 - photo top, left courtesy of istockphoto; photo, bottom courtesy of REAL LOG HOMES®, realloghomes.com, Photographer Rich Frutchey; page 181 - photo courtesy of REAL LOG HOMES®, realloghomes.com, photographer James Ray Spahn; page 202 - top, plan #002D-4506 on page 227, bottom, left and right, plan #002D-4515 on page 225, photos courtesy of CPI, Black & Decker; page 203, both photos courtesy of CPI, Black & Decker.